BOOK 6 MUSICAL CLICHÉS

Series devised by
Maureen Hanke

Book 6 compiled by
Will Taylor
with Elizabeth Bray
and John Stephens

A&C BLACK • LONDON

BOOK CONTENTS

Introduction 4
About *Music Express Year 7* 5
Musical clichés: outline 10
LESSON 1 Introducing musical clichés 12
LESSON 2 Bass ostinato and melody 20
LESSON 3 Adding a drone 26
LESSON 4 Hits and percussion 32
LESSON 5 Completing the structure 40
LESSON 6 Performance 46
Gladiator demo score 52
Glossary 54
Acknowledgements 56

AUDIO CD TRACK LIST

TRACK	CONTENT
1	Extract from *The Society Raffles* by Stephen Chadwick
2	Extract from *On earth as it is in heaven* from *The Mission* by Ennio Morricone
3	Extract from *Movement 1* from *Mythodea* by Vangelis
4	*Gladiator demo* by Will Taylor
5	*Gladiator demo* bass ostinato
6	*Gladiator demo* bass ostinato copy track
7	*Gladiator demo* bass ostinato + untuned percussion ostinato + timpani ostinato
8	*Gladiator demo* untuned percussion ostinato
9	*Gladiator demo* untuned percussion ostinato copy track
10	*Gladiator demo* timpani ostinato
11	*Gladiator demo* timpani ostinato copy track
12	*Gladiator demo* – composed with midi sounds
13	*Gladiator demo* melody + bass ostinato
14	*Gladiator demo* looped bass ostinato and untuned percussion ostinato
15	*Heroic melody 1* by Will Taylor
16	*Heroic melody 2* by Will Taylor
17	*Heroic melody 3* by Will Taylor
18	*Gladiator demo* melody + bass ostinato + drone
19	*Gladiator demo* drone

CD-ROM CONTENTS

PRESENTATION
Unit overview
Learning intentions lessons 1–6

PRINTOUTS
1. Unit overview
2. Learning intentions lessons 1–6
3. Trailers and their music
4. The symphony orchestra
5. Listening to instruments
5t. Listening to instruments – teacher answer sheet
6. Musical clichés: action film trailers
7. Composing a bass ostinato
8. Research action film composers
9. Composing a bass ostinato – keyboard
10. Composing a bass ostinato using a midi sequencer
11. A typical midi sequencer
12. Composing a heroic melody
13. Key words
14. Composing a heroic melody – keyboard
15. Composing a heroic melody using a midi sequencer
16. Assessment criteria
17. Composition ideas bank
18. Composing guidelines
19. Finishing touches using a midi sequencer
20. Example composition plan
21. Composition plan
22. Programme notes
23. End of unit evaluation sheet

VIDEO CLIPS
1. *Gladiator* teaser trailer accompanied by *The Society Raffles* by Stephen Chadwick
2. *Gladiator* teaser trailer accompanied by *On earth as it is in heaven* from *The Mission* by Ennio Morricone
3. *Gladiator* teaser trailer accompanied by *Movement 1* from *Mythodea* by Vangelis
4. *Gladiator* teaser trailer accompanied by its original music (*Anvil of Crom* by Basil Poledouris)
5. *Gladiator* teaser trailer without accompaniment
6. *Gladiator* teaser trailer accompanied by *Gladiator demo* by Will Taylor

PICTURE GALLERY
Trumpet
French horn
Trombone
Tuba
Timpani

MIDI FILES
gladiator.mid
compose.mid

TEACHER INFORMATION
Sample lesson plan
Using ICT
Using electronic keyboards
Using a midi sequencer
Using this CD-ROM

First published 2006
by A&C Black Publishers Ltd
38 Soho Square, London W1D 3HB
© 2006 A&C Black Publishers Ltd
ISBN 10: 0-7136-7367-2
ISBN 13: 978-0-7136-7367-8

Teaching text © 2006 Will Taylor, Elizabeth Bray and John Stephens
CD/CD-ROM compilation © ℗ 2006 A&C Black
Edited by Emily Wilson, Rebecca Taylor and Harriet Lowe
Inside design by James Watson, Susan McIntyre, Jocelyn Lucas and Carla Moss. Cover design by Jocelyn Lucas
CD-ROM interface design by Tatiana Demidova
Cover illustration © 2005 Graham Hutchings
Inside illustrations © 2006 Kanako Damerum and Yuzuru Takasaki
Music setting by Jeanne Roberts
Audio CD sound engineering by Stephen Chadwick at 3D Music Ltd

Video clips edited by Jamie Acton-Bond at AB Video Productions
CD-ROM post-production by Ian Shepherd and Karen Manning at Sound Recording Technology

A&C Black uses paper produced with elemental chlorine-free pulp, harvested from managed sustainable forests.

All rights reserved.
Only material marked photocopiable may be freely photocopied for educational purposes for use in the school or educational establishment for which it was purchased. Any material not marked photocopiable may not be photocopied. No part of this publication may be reproduced in any form or by any means – photographic, electronic or mechanical, including recording, taping or information storage and retrieval systems – without the prior permission in writing of the publishers.

A CIP catalogue record for this book is available from the British Library.

INTRODUCTION

Musical clichés is the final unit in the *Music Express Year 7* series. It combines both listening and composing activities to introduce pupils to the musical clichés and conventions associated with action film trailers.

This half term unit of work is divided into six coherent and clearly structured lessons. Each lesson is 50 minutes long, with extension activities for schools with more time available, and progresses in a controlled and challenging way.

Pupils are introduced to the concept of musical clichés and conventions and learn to identify those associated with the action film genre. They listen to different film soundtracks and complete workshop-style activities based around *Gladiator demo*, a piece specially composed by Will Taylor to fit a clip from the teaser trailer for the film, *Gladiator*. They then compose and perform their own piece of music to accompany the trailer clip, using the clichés they have learnt, and evaluate their own work and the work of others against clearly described objectives.

Activities and resources are provided for using acoustic instruments, electronic keyboards and ICT, as suits the needs and set-up of each school.

The activities are described in the book; the CD and CD-ROM provide all the supporting material and resources needed for each lesson.

ABOUT THE SERIES AUTHOR

Maureen Hanke MA BMus is the head of Norfolk Education Service. She started her career as a music teacher in the East End of London. Later, as a music adviser, she developed a national reputation for music education workshops and became Head of Music Education at Trinity College of Music. Her work has involved PGCE training, QCA consultation and more recently she devised *Music Express*, an award-winning school resource.

ABOUT THE AUTHORS OF MUSICAL CLICHÉS

Will Taylor is currently Assistant Principal and Head of Creative, Expressive and Aesthetic Studies at The Northampton Academy. He is a lead practitioner for music for the Specialist Schools and Academies Trust and is a regular secondary music education consultant to the Qualifications and Curriculum Authority (QCA).

Elizabeth Bray worked for several years as Head of Music at Daventry William Parker School before taking up the post of Advanced Skills Teacher for Music at The Priory LSST in Lincoln, where she is also involved in county initiatives. She has written several articles on music education and worked as an OFSTED inspector.

John Stephens has taught music at all levels for almost twenty years in the London boroughs of Greenwich, Lewisham and Southwark. He has also produced music commercially, acted as a consultant for Lewisham's New Opportunities Fund (NoF) ICT training for secondary music teachers, and is currently Co-ordinator of Greenwich Music Service.

ABOUT THE COMPOSER OF GLADIATOR DEMO

Will Taylor has composed and arranged music for a variety of educational events. This has included music for the Specialist Schools and Academies Trust conference at Tate Britain in 2001, and a choral arrangement performed by massed school choirs from across the Specialist Schools network at Symphony Hall, Birmingham, in 2004.

ABOUT MUSIC EXPRESS YEAR 7

Music Express Year 7 provides teaching activities that are imaginative, inspiring and fun. It is user-friendly, well planned, fully resourced and based on good practice for teaching and learning. It promotes inclusion, draws upon a range of music from diverse cultures and enables all pupils to build on their already established skills and knowledge in a purposeful and engaging way.

Each book provides a unit of six weekly lessons, which are intended to be taught over a half term. Each lesson follows the same pattern: objectives are identified and shared with the pupils and the lesson then unfolds through clear activities delivered in a range of styles. The lessons are clearly set out into starter (focus), core activities and plenary, and each lesson provides a suggestion for appropriate homework.

Each lesson is designed to last 50 minutes and approximate timings are provided in the book for each activity.

Suggestions are provided in each lesson for activities which might be used as extension work for students or to extend the lesson for schools with more time available.

This resource offers:

- ways of using a keyboard for appropriate activities;
- ways to incorporate ICT into music teaching and learning;
- extension activities;
- printouts for pupils' files;
- instrumental parts where required;
- all music on CD;
- additional background information on the composers and pieces featured in the activities.

A key feature of the *Music Express Year 7* resource is the use of video clips in which composers and musicians demonstrate and explain their musical thinking. Pupils have the opportunity to reflect on and adopt their thought processes as models for their own learning.

USING MUSIC EXPRESS YEAR 7 AS A SCHEME OF WORK

Music Express Year 7 fulfils the requirements of the Music National Curriculum of England, of Wales and of Northern Ireland and supports the 5-14 National Guidelines for Scotland.

It is inspired and informed by units in the QCA Key Stage 3 scheme of work, but the programmes do not necessarily follow the units exactly. The QCA expectations and lesson objectives are embedded in the units which are designed to enable pupils to meet the standards expected of levels 4 and 5.

The series has been written and created to support high quality teaching and learning and to raise the standards of achievement in music at Key Stage 3. Lessons throughout the unit include reference to:

- the use of evidence and dialogue to identify where pupils are in their musical learning, where they need to go and how best to get there;
- the opportunity for pupils to identify what needs improving and how they can do so;
- peer and self assessment;
- analysis and evaluation of musicians in action to help develop the competence and confidence of every learner;
- clear indication of managing music lessons in a range of whole class, group and individual teaching and learning situations;
- ICT strategies.

Each unit has all the content required for each lesson leaving the teacher to focus on their teaching skills.

THE UNITS

There are six units in *Music Express Year 7*, published as six separate Book + CD + CD-ROM packs. Below is a list of the titles available in the series:

BOOK 1: BRIDGING UNIT (LINKS TO QCA UNIT 1)

Bridging unit is a composing unit that builds on the vast range of musical experiences in Year 6 and is designed, therefore, to help address the wide range of skills, knowledge and understanding that pupils bring to Year 7.

Pupils work initially with simple rhythmic and melodic patterns and, following a workshop style, they use improvisation as a means to composition. Through a commissioned piece of music, pupils listen to and observe the composing process, and in a series of video clips showing an interview with the composer, they gain an insight into his creative thinking. Pupils complete a composition and are able to consider the strengths of their work against clearly described assessment criteria and set their own targets for future learning.

BOOK 2: PERFORMING TOGETHER (PROGRESSES FROM YEAR 5/6 UNIT 20)

This unit develops and demonstrates pupils' ability to prepare and take part in a large group performance. It provides an opportunity for pupils to maintain and develop the invaluable skills of learning by ear, reading simple notation, rehearsing a part and working as an ensemble. All parts are available on the CD and CD-ROM. Principles of preparation unfold throughout the unit and the flexibility of the material provided (eg opportunities for two-part singing, solo spots, improvisation and simple movement/dance routines) ensures that everyone can be included.

The unit is an important foundation for work in arranging and song writing later in the year. It also provides a useful basis for those pupils wanting to start a band or group out of school, who will need to learn how to rehearse and perform the songs they want to play.

BOOK 3: MUSICAL CYCLES (WEST AFRICA) (LINKS TO QCA UNIT 4)

Musical cycles (West Africa) combines performing, listening and composition activities to explore the structures and key characteristics of West African music and its instruments. Teaching and learning are illustrated through video clips and clearly described workshop activities that explore musical cycles, signals and rhythmic and melodic improvisation. Listening is integral to the work and CD extracts include a traditional rhythm from Guinea/Sierra Leone, and recordings of performances by Mamady Keïta and the Malian singer, Oumou Sangaré. The unit unfolds to enable pupils either to complete a composition activity, modelled by a professional composer, or to prepare a performance of *Djolé*.

BOOK 4: MUSICAL STRUCTURES (LINKS TO QCA UNIT 2)

In this unit, pupils learn about the principles of repetition and contrast that underpin ternary and rondo forms in Western European music. In the context of dance music from the past to the present, pupils are guided towards a basic understanding of simple harmony and tonality, allowing them to construct their own pieces in ternary and rondo form.

BOOK 5: ARRANGING MUSIC (LINKS TO QCA UNIT 6)

Building on the *Performing together* unit (*Music Express Year 7 Book 2*) pupils learn about arranging techniques through listening to, arranging and performing a traditional spiritual and an original spiritual-style composition.

Pupils learn about the key tools of arranging, revisiting chords and encountering instrumentation. They are guided through an arrangement and then create their own, enabling them to develop critical judgements on the characteristics both of their own arrangement and those of others.

BOOK 6: MUSICAL CLICHÉS (LINKS TO QCA UNIT 5)

Musical clichés is the last of the six units – the finale to the *Music Express Year 7* series. The unit develops pupils' ability to recognise, analyse and use a range of musical clichés used in a specific musical genre.

Pupils are introduced to the musical clichés and conventions used in action film music through listening to and analysing extracts from different film soundtracks and completing workshop-style activities based around a piece of music specially composed for the unit. Using the clichés they have learnt, they then compose and perform their own piece of music to fit an extract from a teaser trailer from the blockbuster action film, *Gladiator*.

Please note – we have not included a separate Soundscapes (ICT) unit: instead we have integrated ICT into each unit by offering the opportunity to develop objectives through ICT, electronic keyboards and/or classroom instruments and acoustic instruments.

PREPARATION AND PLANNING

Music Express Year 7 Book 6 is designed to minimise preparation time.

Learning objectives and outcomes are given at the start of each lesson. **Teaching tips** also provide differentiation and assessment, and there is an exemplar lesson plan on the CD-ROM.

The unit and lesson aims are provided on the CD-ROM both in a **presentation** and on printouts for the teacher to view with the pupils. The assessment criteria are also provided as a printout on the CD-ROM.

A complete list of resources is given at the start of each lesson. Key words are highlighted in bold in the activity text when they are first introduced and their definitions are given on each page under **Key words**. There is a glossary at the back of the book and a printout of key words is also provided for pupils on the CD-ROM.

Icons next to the activity headings indicate what you will need to prepare:

- Printouts icon: some activities require worksheets or background information to be printed out from the CD-ROM.

- Optional printouts icon: for some activities worksheets are suggested but are not essential to the activity.

- CD icon: details which audio tracks are required.

- Optional CD icon: for some activities audio tracks are suggested but are not essential to the activity.

- Video clips icon: you will need to have a computer and data projector set up to show the video clips.

- Optional video clips icon: for some activities a video clip is suggested but is not essential to the activity. You will need to have a computer and data projector set up to show the video clips.

- Midi files icon: indicates that midi files are required. You will need to have a midi sequencer installed on your computer, eg Cubasis.

- Picture gallery: you can either view pictures on a whiteboard or download printable versions to use in a classroom display or to provide as handouts.

Presentation: you will need to have a computer and data projector or whiteboard set up to show the unit overview and learning intentions for each lesson in a presentation on the CD-ROM.

Other resources required are listed under **Resources** in the book at the start of each lesson.

CLASSROOM MANAGEMENT

Music Express Year 7 is designed to enhance and support individual teaching styles. It is not intended to dictate paradigms or pedagogy but rather to make suggestions. Each lesson includes suggestions for managing the activities, including ideas for whole class teaching, small group teaching and giving opportunities to individuals to show leadership and to work on their own. How the activities are managed may need to be adapted to meet the physical environments and cultures of individual schools. Lessons towards the end of each unit expect pupils to demonstrate more independence in the personal management of their learning as the questions and tasks become generally more open.

Each lesson contains many more ideas and much more information than would be expected to be included in a 50-minute teaching period. The lessons are rich in extension activities, alternative keyboard activities, ICT activities and extra background information. When teachers are selecting activities and material, they should bear in mind that all pupils must be able to advance their musical skills, knowledge and understanding. For example it may not be appropriate to give all the background information for all the CD extracts on first using them, as this might interrupt the flow of the lesson. However, the information is available for use at an appropriate point in the unit.

Notation is introduced and used throughout the units in accordance with the lesson objectives and learning outcomes. It is for the teacher to decide if using notation is appropriate for their pupils and to adapt the content of the lesson accordingly, either by increasing the use of conventional notation or by increasing the amount of music learnt by ear.

ASSESSMENT

Music Express Year 7 has several layers of assessment. As an initial support, Teaching tips are provided throughout each lesson. These give further clarification of aspects of the lesson and points that might be of particular benefit to the new teacher. At the end of each lesson there is a summary of points for assessment. These, together with the plenary sessions, combine to provide an ongoing picture of whole class development. They provide an opportunity for the pupils and the teacher to decide what stage the pupils are at in their learning, where they need to go and how best to get there. Major pieces of work towards the end of each unit have an assessment sheet supporting the National Curriculum level descriptions and an opportunity for self, peer and teacher assessment to consider the quality of the work. These build to give a profile of progress for each pupil. Each unit includes an end of unit evaluation that pupils have the opportunity to complete.

SINGING

Music Express Year 7 does not provide instruction on using the voice – however, warm-up exercises and guidance are provided. Do remind pupils to put as little pressure on the throat as possible and instead support the sound with air from the diaphragm. Often pupils sing from the throat – forcing the air in this way can easily lead to cracked notes or neck strain, particularly in the adolescent voice. Singing from the diaphragm should create a warm, rich sound with extensive dynamic possibilities.

It is a common mistake to put less effort into singing quietly. Remind singers to use more air and greater effort to support a quiet note. In this way they will be able to make a quiet note that is both potent and sustained.

Some pupils will find it hard to pitch a note accurately. *Music Express Year 7* frequently uses a call and response format, as it gives pupils less time to worry. Being able to hear a tune in their heads first will also help pupils to vocalise the internal sound correctly.

A warm-up is a useful and important activity to avoid strained voices and to get pupils in the right frame of mind for singing. An effective activity is to use the letter 'F' sound. Take a deep breath and start the sound slowly, gradually quickening, like a steam engine pulling away from the platform. Encourage the pupils to feel the push from their diaphragm and to watch and feel their own stomachs going in and out.

ICT

Many of the activities in *Music Express Year 7* will benefit from the use of a computer and whiteboard to display the supporting materials found on the CD-ROM.

In addition, some activities have specific ICT activities, details of which can be found at the end of each lesson.

Some of the ICT activities are led by the teacher from the front of the class using a whiteboard, for example, using a karaoke player in Books 2 and 5. For these activities make sure that the computer's sound output is connected to a classroom hi-fi (or equivalent), so that pupils can hear clearly while they clap rhythms or sing.

Some of the ICT activities require pupils to work independently in groups, for example using a midi sequencer in Books 1, 5 and 6. This might make it necessary for the group using the computer to use headphones, if, for example, the rest of the class is working in groups with their instruments in the same area. Some music departments will have more than one computer, in which case teachers may be able to involve more groups in the ICT activities.

All the ICT activities should be deliverable on either a PC or a Mac computer. Software guidance is given on the CD-ROM.

ELECTRONIC KEYBOARDS

Many schools are equipped with electronic keyboards and many pupils will relish the idea of learning to play the keyboard. The keyboard's functions can easily be taught and exploited to achieve musical learning objectives. Laying down the foundations of good technique is an important aspect of Year 7 keyboard work. In *Music Express Year 7* keyboard tuition starts from the very beginning, providing materials to demonstrate good hand positions, emphasising the importance of developing both hands in playing and establishing an understanding of fingering.

One keyboard per pupil is the ideal situation, but if pupils are sharing, ensure that partners swap places regularly.

Each unit provides activities both for the beginner and more confident player, but teachers must remember that each unit has higher expectations of achievement and any pupils who miss the earlier units may miss some important developmental work.

Fingering is suggested throughout the unit, but it can be changed, or at times ignored, if it becomes too much of an impediment to the creative process.

It is not practical to discuss here the many brands and models of keyboard available in such a fast developing market. However, *Music Express Year 7* does assume that the keyboards which schools use will support some basic functions: eg timbre, tempo, style and volume. The facility to record will also be invaluable.

Please note that teaching activity time does not include familiarising yourself with keyboard functionality and ICT software and, depending on experience, you might need to allow extra planning time to do this.

MUSICAL CLICHÉS: OUTLINE

Lesson 1 Introducing musical clichés

OBJECTIVES
By the end of the lesson pupils should:
- know the purpose of a film trailer and its music;
- understand the concept of a musical cliché;
- understand the role of the bass ostinato in music for action film trailers.

OUTCOMES
Pupils:
- identify musical conventions and clichés associated with this genre;
- learn to play example ostinati.
- compose their own bass ostinato for an action film trailer.

Lesson 2 Bass ostinato and melody

OBJECTIVES
By the end of the lesson pupils should:
- understand the role of the heroic melody cliché;
- be able to develop melodic ideas and combine them with the bass ostinato;
- understand the importance of the first and fifth notes of a scale in music for action film trailers.

OUTCOMES
Pupils:
- compose their own heroic melody ideas to fit with their bass ostinato;
- perform their ideas in front of the class.

Lesson 3 Adding a drone

OBJECTIVES
By the end of the lesson pupils should:
- understand the role of each instrumental part and its relationship to the others in their composition;
- understand the role of the drone cliché.

OUTCOMES
Pupils:
- continue to develop ideas for their heroic melody, and compose a suitable drone;
- perform their musical ideas in time with each other.

Lesson 4 Hits and percussion

OBJECTIVES
By the end of the lesson pupils should:
- be confident about performing their musical ideas;
- understand the role of the hits cliché and percussion clichés.

OUTCOMES
Pupils:
- introduce hits and percussion into their composition;
- perform and discuss their work in progress.

Lesson 5 Completing the structure

OBJECTIVES
By the end of the lesson pupils should:
- understand how to structure their ideas;
- understand the purpose of writing down a musical structure.

OUTCOMES
Pupils:
- are able to structure their music to fit the mood of the trailer;
- are able to make a simple score of their composition.

Lesson 6 Performance

OBJECTIVES
By the end of the lesson pupils should:
- understand the clichés used in music for action film trailers;
- be able to perform their composition to the rest of the class.

OUTCOMES
Pupils:
- perform their composition in front of their class in time with the trailer;
- assess and evaluate their own and other pupils' compositions.

Lesson 1 Introducing musical clichés

Focus
1. Learn about the purpose of film trailers and their music
2. Learn about the instruments used in music to accompany action film trailers
3. Learn about the bass ostinato cliché in music for action film trailers `>> KEYBOARD >> ICT`
4. Pupils compose their own bass ostinato `>> KEYBOARD >> ICT`

Plenary

Lesson 2 Bass ostinato and melody

Focus
1. Revise the bass ostinati composed last lesson `>> KEYBOARD >> ICT`
2. Pupils learn about the heroic melody cliché
3. Pupils begin composing a heroic melody to fit with their bass ostinato `>> KEYBOARD >> ICT`
4. Pupils perform their heroic melody ideas to the class

Plenary

Lesson 3 Adding a drone

Focus
1. Pupils are set their composition task
2. Pupils review their bass ostinato and develop their heroic melody ideas `>> KEYBOARD >> ICT`
3. Pupils learn about the drone cliché
4. Groups add a drone to their bass ostinato and heroic melody `>> KEYBOARD >> ICT`

Plenary

Lesson 4 Hits and percussion

Focus
1. Pupils learn about the hits cliché `>> ICT`
2. Groups revise their work from last lesson and explore adding hits to their composition `>> KEYBOARD >> ICT`
3. Pupils learn about the timpani and untuned percussion clichés `>> ICT`
4. Pupils continue working on their composition `>> KEYBOARD >> ICT`

Plenary

Lesson 5 Completing the structure

Focus
1. Pupils revise their composition `>> KEYBOARD`
2. Discuss ideas for structuring the composition `>> ICT`
3. Groups develop the structure of their composition `>> KEYBOARD >> ICT`
4. Pupils finalise their composition plan `>> ICT`

Plenary

Lesson 6 Performance

Focus
1. Pupils rehearse their composition with the *Gladiator* trailer `>> KEYBOARD >> ICT`
2. Groups perform their composition to the class `>> KEYBOARD >> ICT`
3. Groups assess their composition `>> KEYBOARD >> ICT`

Plenary

Lesson 1 — Introducing musical clichés

OBJECTIVES
By the end of the lesson pupils should:
- know the purpose of a film trailer and its music;
- understand the concept of a musical cliché;
- understand the role of the bass ostinato in music for action film trailers.

OUTCOMES
Pupils:
- identify musical conventions and clichés associated with this genre;
- learn to play example ostinati;
- compose their own bass ostinato for an action film trailer.

RESOURCES

AUDIO CD
Tracks 1–11

CD-ROM
- Presentation
- Video clips 1–5
- Printouts 1–11
- Picture gallery
- Midi files (optional)
- Teacher information (optional)

INSTRUMENTS
- A selection of tuned and untuned instruments (optional)
- Timpani tuned to D and A (optional)
- Electronic keyboards (optional)

ICT
- Whiteboard or computer and data projector with sound
- Midi sequencer software (optional)

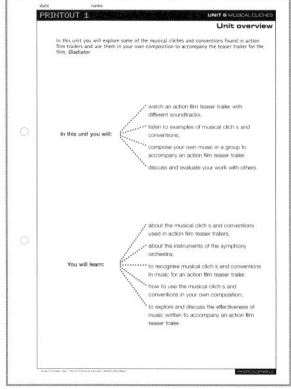

Printout 1: Unit overview

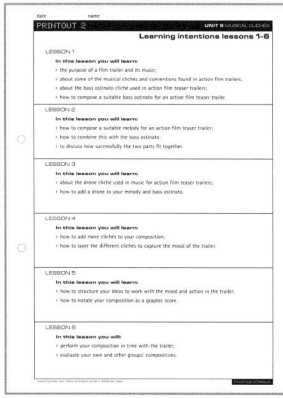

Printout 2: Learning intentions lessons 1–6

Focus
5 mins — video 1–3 — audio 1–3 — printouts 1, 2 — Presentation

- Introduce this unit using the presentation on the CD-ROM or printout 1.

- Watch the *Gladiator* teaser trailer extract with three different soundtracks (video clips 1–3). Ask the pupils which they think is the correct soundtrack and why *(eg soundtrack 3 most closely matches the mood of the trailer)*.

- Explain that none of the soundtracks is the actual one, but that soundtrack 3 contains certain musical ideas that we associate with this type of film trailer, therefore making it sound suitable.

- Display the learning intentions for this lesson using the presentation on the CD-ROM or printout 2.

TEACHING TIP
The soundtracks for video clips 1–3 are also provided on the audio CD (tracks 1–3): soundtrack 1 was composed to accompany the silent movie, *The Society Raffles*; soundtrack 2 is *On earth as it is in heaven* from *The Mission*; soundtrack 3 is from *Mythodea, music for the NASA mission: 2001 mars odyssey* (see CD track list, page 2).

1 Learn about the purpose of film trailers and their music
10 mins — video 4, 5 — printout 3

- As a class, discuss the purpose of a film trailer *(eg to advertise the film and provide information about the type of film, the plot, the cast, the director and the release date)*.

- Explain the difference between teaser and theatrical trailers and their music, using **Trailers and their music** (printout 3).

- Watch the *Gladiator* teaser trailer extract with the real soundtrack (video clip 4). Discuss the role the music plays in the trailer *(eg it captures the mood of the film and contributes to the trailer's success)*.

- Discuss how the music in video clip 4 captures the mood of the trailer *(eg there is a large orchestral sound, dramatic use of brass and percussion timbres, driving rhythms and loud dynamics building to a climax as the word 'Gladiator' appears on the screen at the end)*.

LESSON 1
INTRODUCING MUSICAL CLICHÉS

TEACHING TIPS

You might like to watch the silent *Gladiator* trailer (video clip 5) as a comparison with the original *Gladiator* trailer (video clip 4) to help the pupils hear what the music adds to the trailer.

Video clip 4 is an extract from a teaser trailer for the film, *Gladiator* and uses music from the film, *Conan the Barbarian* (see printout 3).

Printout 3 also provides background information about the film, *Gladiator*.

KEY WORDS

musical cliché – a phrase or convention which is overused in a particular genre of music and is therefore predictable. From the French 'clicher', meaning 'to stereotype'.

genre – a type or category. Pop, folk, classical and jazz are all musical genres.

ostinato – a short repeated rhythmic or melodic pattern.

2 Learn about the instruments used in music to accompany action film trailers

10 mins ● 4 4 5 5t ▢

- Explain that music for action film trailers is frequently composed for a symphony orchestra with prominent use of brass instruments and timpani.

- Use the picture gallery on the CD-ROM and *The symphony orchestra* (printout 4) to learn about the instruments of the orchestra and listen to the brass instruments and timpani.

- Listen to *Gladiator demo* (track 4) and ask the class to answer the questions on *Listening to instruments* (printout 5). Replay the track as many times as appropriate.

- Listen to track 4 again and discuss the answers as a class.

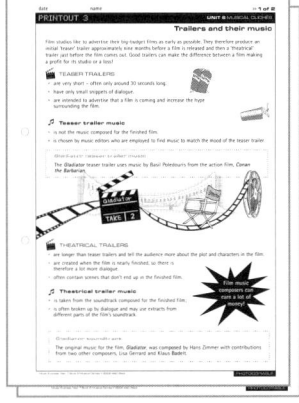

Printout 3: Trailers and their music (2 pages)

TEACHING TIPS

Printout 5t provides sample answers for the teacher, if required.

It may be helpful to listen to the brass instruments and timpani using the picture gallery on the CD-ROM in-between extracts, to help pupils recognise the sounds.

Gladiator demo (track 4) was composed especially for this unit by the author, Will Taylor.

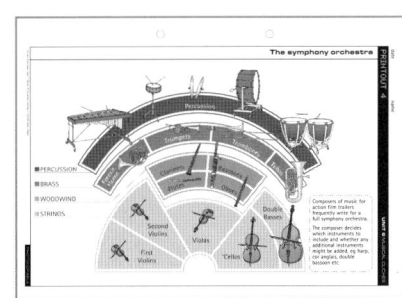

Printout 4: The symphony orchestra

3 Learn about the bass ostinato cliché in music for action film trailers

▶ KEYBOARD page 16   ▶ ICT page 18

10 mins ● 5–11 6

- Display *Musical clichés: action film trailers* (printout 6). Explain that these are the action film trailer musical clichés the pupils will be learning about in this unit. Explain the terms **musical cliché**, **genre** and **ostinato**.

- Explain that the bass ostinato is the most important cliché, because it supports the whole composition.

- Listen to the bass ostinato from *Gladiator demo* (track 5) on its own and discuss its musical characteristics, eg:
  - it is played on just one note (D);
  - it is very rhythmic with short note values, triplets and syncopation;
  - it is played on low sounding instruments (by 'cellos and double basses on two different Ds, which creates a thick texture).

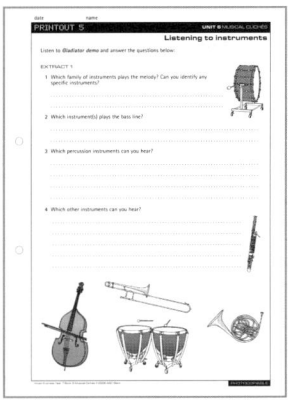

Printout 5: Listening to instruments

13

LESSON 1
INTRODUCING MUSICAL CLICHÉS

KEY WORDS

texture – the number of performers in a piece.

syncopation – instead of accenting the strong beats (eg <u>1</u> 2 <u>3</u> 4), syncopated music accents the weak beats (eg 1 <u>+</u> 2 <u>+</u> 3 <u>+</u> 4 <u>+</u>) or 1 + <u>2</u> + 3 + <u>4</u> +).

triplet – a group of three notes of equal length performed in the time of two.

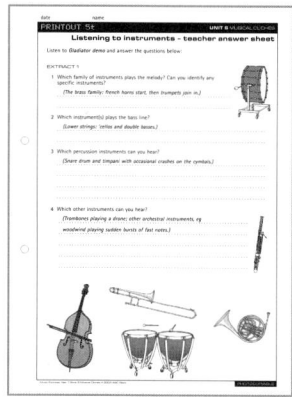

Printout 5t: Listening to instruments – teacher answer sheet

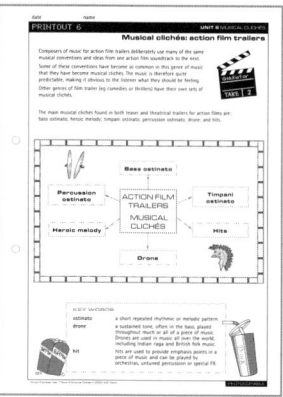

Printout 6: Musical clichés: action film trailers

- Explain the terms **texture**, **syncopation** and **triplet**.

- All learn to play the bass ostinato by ear, with body percussion and voices using the copy track (track 6). (Alternatively, play the ostinato yourself for the pupils to copy.)

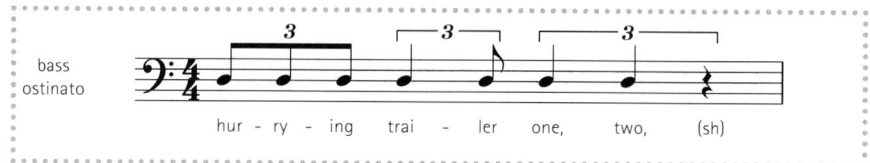

- Once the class are comfortable with the rhythm, let them continue without you or track 6. Then encourage as many pupils as possible to transfer the rhythm onto a tuned instrument, playing it on the note D.

- Explain that the bass ostinato can be punctuated by an additional untuned percussion ostinato and/or timpani ostinato. Listen to how these fit together in *Gladiator demo* (track 7).

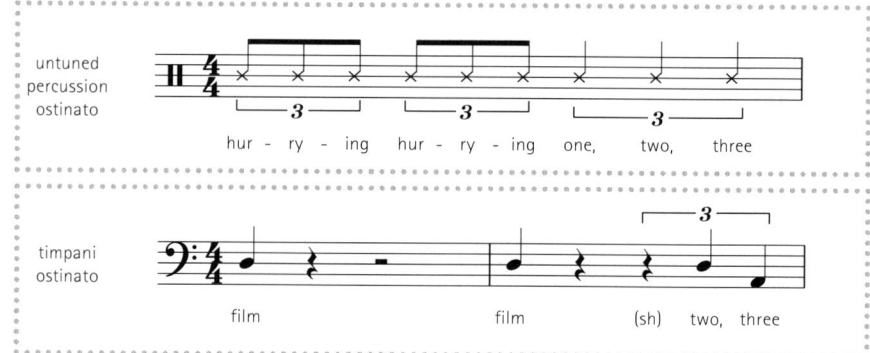

- All learn to play these ostinati as pupils did the bass ostinato, using tracks 8–9 for the untuned percussion ostinato and tracks 10–11 for the timpani ostinato. (Alternatively, play the ostinati yourself for the pupils to copy.)

- Divide the class into three groups to perform the three ostinati together:
  - the first group starts repeating the bass ostinato;
  - when it is settled, the second group joins in repeating the untuned percussion ostinato;
  - finally, the third group joins in repeating the timpani ostinato.

- Discuss the effect of the combined ostinati, eg:
  - the bass ostinato is emphasised by the untuned percussion and timpani;
  - the combined ostinati help to drive the music forward;
  - the bass ostinato supports the untuned percussion and timpani ostinati.

TEACHING TIPS

The word rhythms provided on this page will be used in the next activity to help pupils compose their own ostinati and may be useful here to help pupils internalise the rhythms.

Pupils without suitable instruments should use body percussion and voices, or should swap places regularly.

LESSON 1
INTRODUCING MUSICAL CLICHÉS

4 Pupils compose their own bass ostinato

KEYBOARD page 17   **ICT** page 19

10 mins [7]

- Distribute copies of *Composing a bass ostinato* (printout 7). Go through the printout with your class, practising speaking the rhythm patterns provided in time with a steady pulse. Explain the term **staccato**.

- Divide the class into pairs to compose their own bass ostinato on the note D to accompany the *Gladiator* teaser trailer. They should invent a suitable spoken rhythm pattern with their voices at first and then transfer it onto any bass instruments available.

- Each pair practises repeating their bass ostinato rhythmically, until they can play it confidently.

- Invite as many pairs as possible to demonstrate their bass ostinati and ask the class to comment on how effective each would be at capturing the mood of the *Gladiator* trailer.

- Pupils make a note of their ostinato in the space provided on printout 7.

EXTENSION ACTIVITY
Ask pupils to experiment with using more than one note for their bass ostinato. You might like to limit them to the notes D and A, or notes from the scale DEFGABCD.

Make sure pupils write down the note names under their rhythm pattern on printout 7, to remember for next lesson.

TEACHING TIP
Circulate around the class as they work and help pupils to practise their bass ostinato in time with a steady pulse.

KEY WORDS
staccato – notes which are played short and detached.

ASSESSMENT FOR LEARNING
- Who can use the new terminology in response to questions?
- Who demonstrates a strong sense of pulse and rhythm when performing the ostinati?

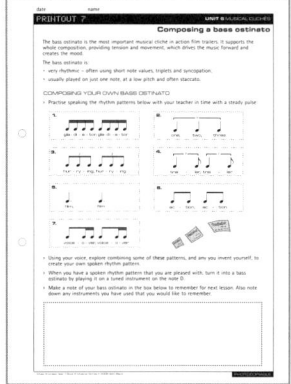

Printout 7: Composing a bass ostinato

Plenary
5 mins

- Revise the purpose of a film trailer and its music and what is meant by the term, musical cliché.

- Revise the musical clichés associated with action film trailers.

LESSON 1
INTRODUCING MUSICAL CLICHÉS

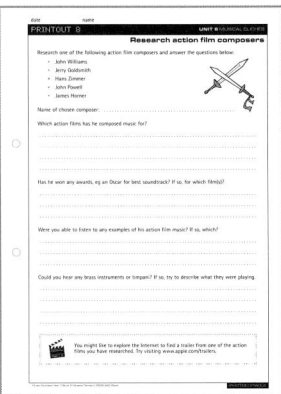

Printout 8: Research action film composers

Homework

- Pupils research an action film trailer composer using the Internet and complete *Research action film composers* (printout 8). They should try to listen to some examples of their music and particularly for any brass instruments or timpani being played.

- Ask pupils to bring in instruments from home to the next lesson, particularly any brass or bass instruments.

TEACHING TIP
The website referred to on the printout was suitable at the time of publication. It provides a good bank of trailers, should you wish to choose a different action film trailer for the pupils to compose music for.

KEYBOARD (see page 13)

3 Learn about the bass ostinato cliché in music for action film trailers

10 mins ● 5–11 📄 6

- Introduce the bass ostinato cliché, as described on pages 13–14.

- Demonstrate the bass ostinato from *Gladiator demo* using a keyboard, then ask the pupils to join in using body percussion or voices. (Alternatively, use the bass ostinato copy track – track 6).

- Once the class are confident with the rhythm, encourage as many pupils as possible to transfer the rhythm onto the note D on a keyboard. They might like to use the metronome function to play in time with a steady pulse, eg 80 beats per minute (bpm).

- Revise how to change the voice on a keyboard and encourage pupils to select an appropriate voice for their bass ostinato.

- Explain that the bass ostinato cliché is often punctuated by an untuned percussion ostinato and/or timpani ostinato. Listen to how these fit together in *Gladiator demo* (track 7).

- Teach the untuned percussion ostinato then the timpani ostinato to the class using tracks 8–11, or by playing the ostinati yourself for pupils to copy.

- Divide the class into three groups to perform these ostinati together, as described on page 14. (Alternatively, if your pupils are working in pairs at the keyboard and your keyboard allows, suggest they record the bass ostinato and then perform the untuned percussion and timpani ostinati live over the top.)

TEACHING TIPS
The word rhythms shown on page 14 will be used in the next activity to help pupils compose their own ostinati and may be useful here to help the pupils internalise these rhythms.
Encourage more advanced pupils to alternate the fingers they use to play the ostinati.

RETURN TO ACTIVITY 4   (page 15)

LESSON 1
INTRODUCING MUSICAL CLICHÉS

KEYBOARD (see page 15)

4 Pupils compose their own bass ostinato

10 mins [9]

- Distribute copies of *Composing a bass ostinato – keyboard* (printout 9), and go through it with the class. Practise speaking the rhythm patterns provided, then demonstrate transferring them onto the keyboard on the note D.

- Explain the term **staccato**.

- Each pair practises repeating their bass ostinato rhythmically over and over at a steady tempo (eg 80 bpm).

- Invite as many pairs as possible to demonstrate their bass ostinati to the class and ask pupils to comment on how effective each would be at capturing the mood of the *Gladiator* trailer.

- Pupils make a note of their ostinato in the space provided on printout 9, making sure they include details of the voice they have chosen.

EXTENSION ACTIVITY

Ask pupils to experiment with using more than one note for their bass ostinato. You might like to limit them to the notes D and A, or notes from the scale DEFGABCD.

Make sure pupils write down the note names under their rhythm pattern on printout 9, to remember for next lesson.

TEACHING TIPS

Circulate around the class as they work and help pupils to practise their bass ostinato in time to a steady pulse.

Encourage pupils to explore the many bass voices available on their keyboard for their ostinato.

RETURN TO PLENARY (page 15)

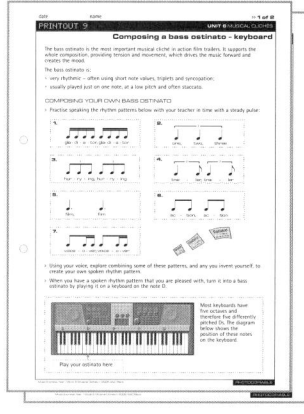

Printout 9: Composing a bass ostinato – keyboard (2 pages)

LESSON 1
INTRODUCING MUSICAL CLICHÉS

ICT (see page 13)

3 Learn about the bass ostinato cliché in music for action film trailers

10 mins · 5, 7–11 · 6 · MIDI

- For this activity you will need a midi sequencer installed on your classroom computer, with the display projected onto a screen or whiteboard and the sound output of the computer enabled.

- Load the file *gladiator.mid* into the sequencer, and make sure it can be heard clearly over the computer's sound system. (See *Using a midi sequencer* in the Teacher information section of the CD-ROM for further information.)

- Introduce the bass ostinato cliché, as described on pages 13–14.

- Use *gladiator.mid* to help the pupils learn the bass ostinato, untuned percussion ostinato and timpani ostinato:

  • select the bass ostinato track and open the edit window;

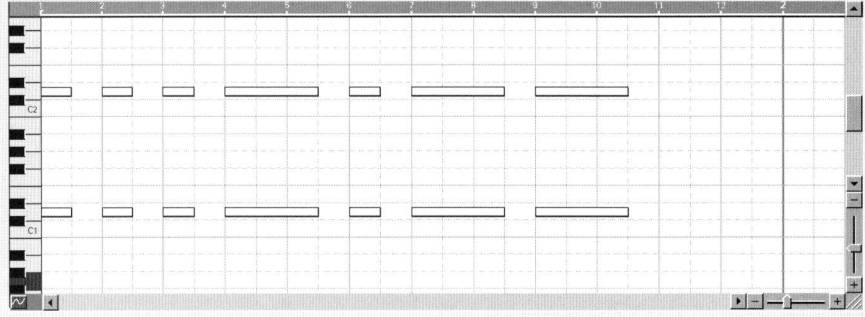

  • play the file and ask the pupils to follow the notes as they scroll by;
  • teach the class to play the ostinato as described on page 14, using the midi file as an audio and visual aid;
  • explain that the bass ostinato cliché is often punctuated by an additional untuned percussion ostinato and/or timpani ostinato;
  • demonstrate these three parts together in the sequencer then teach the untuned percussion and timpani ostinati in turn.

- Divide the class into three groups to perform these ostinati together, then discuss the effect, as described on page 14.

TEACHING TIPS

Explain that a midi file uses the computer or keyboard to produce the sounds, which is why it sounds different to track 5.

Explain that the bass ostinato is played on two different Ds, which is why there are two layers of notes in the sequencer window.

Ask those without suitable instruments to use body percussion and voices when learning each ostinato, and use the metronome click in the sequencer to help with timing, if required.

You might like to use tracks 7–11 to help teach the pupils the untuned percussion and timpani ostinati.

« RETURN TO ACTIVITY 4   (page 15)

LESSON 1
INTRODUCING MUSICAL CLICHÉS

ICT (see page 15)

4 Pupils compose their own bass ostinato
10 mins — 10, 11, MIDI

- Before starting this activity, load the file *compose.mid* into the sequencer and make sure that it can be heard clearly over the computer's sound system. (See *Using a midi sequencer* in the Teacher information section of the CD-ROM for more information.)

- Choose a group of pupils to use the sequencer to compose their own bass ostinato and give them copies of *Composing a bass ostinato using a midi sequencer* (printout 10) and *A typical midi sequencer* (printout 11).

- Go through printout 10 with the group, making sure they follow the instructions to:
  - first familiarise themselves with the sequencer by playing back and looping the *Gladiator demo* bass ostinato, which is provided;
  - next, open the edit window and delete the notes of the *Gladiator demo* bass ostinato to give them a blank track to compose in;
  - then begin composing their own bass ostinato using the pen tool to input notes in the edit window.

- Remind pupils to save their bass ostinato when they are happy with it.

- Invite the group to demonstrate their bass ostinato to the class and ask pupils to comment on how effective it would be at capturing the mood of the *Gladiator* trailer.

EXTENSION ACTIVITY
Pupils experiment with using more than one note for their bass ostinato. You might like to limit them to the notes D and A, or notes from the scale DEFGABCD.

TEACHING TIPS
Make sure pupils knows how to change the cursor to the pen and eraser tools.

The file *compose.mid* has been set up for the pupils to compose using triplet patterns like the *Gladiator demo* bass ostinato. For simplicity, this has been done by setting the time signature (next to tempo in the sequencer window) to 12/8. The strong beats therefore fall on beats 1, 4, 7 and 10, allowing subdivision into threes. The time signature can be changed to 4/4 if this is more appropriate for your pupils.

Encourage pupils to invent a word rhythm to fit their ostinato, so they can join in with their voices as the sequencer plays.

« RETURN TO PLENARY (page 15)

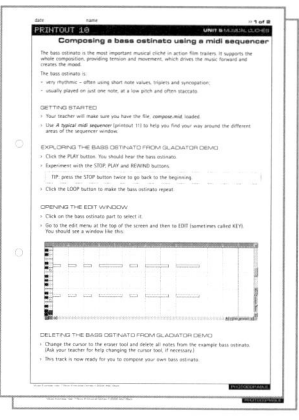

Printout 10: Composing a bass ostinato using a midi sequencer (2 pages)

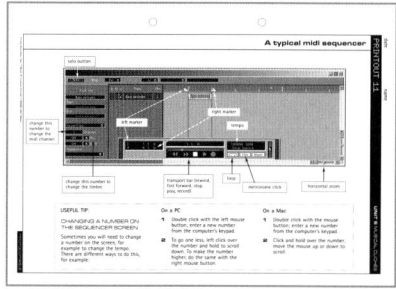

Printout 11: A typical midi sequencer

Lesson 2 — Bass ostinato and melody

OBJECTIVES
By the end of the lesson pupils should:
- understand the role of the heroic melody cliché;
- be able to develop melodic ideas and combine them with the bass ostinato;
- understand the importance of the first and fifth notes of a scale in music for action film trailers.

OUTCOMES
Pupils:
- compose their own heroic melody ideas to fit with their bass ostinato;
- perform their ideas in front of the class.

RESOURCES

AUDIO CD
Tracks 5, 12–17

CD-ROM
- Presentation
- Video clips 3, 4, 6
- Printouts 2, 7–10, 12–15
- Midi files (optional)
- Teacher information (optional)

INSTRUMENTS
- Untuned and tuned instruments (optional)
- Pupils bring in instruments from home (optional)
- Electronic keyboards (optional)

ICT
- Whiteboard or computer and data projector with sound
- Midi sequencer software and midi keyboard (optional)

Printout 2: Learning intentions lessons 1–6

Focus
5 mins — Presentation

- Invite pupils to talk briefly about the composers of music for action film trailers they researched for homework *(eg Hans Zimmer, Jerry Goldsmith, John Williams)*, using the notes they made on **Research action film composers** (printout 8).

- Explain that in this lesson pupils will work in groups to begin to compose music to accompany the *Gladiator* teaser trailer and that their piece will use the clichés associated with action film trailer music to create the right mood.

- Introduce the learning intentions for this lesson using the presentation on the CD-ROM or printout 2.

1 Revise the bass ostinati composed last lesson

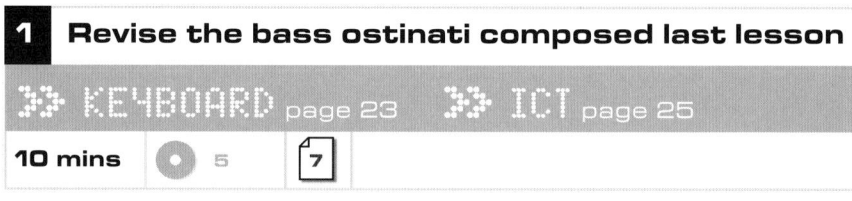

KEYBOARD page 23   **ICT** page 25

10 mins   5   7

- Revise the role of the bass ostinato in music for action film trailers *(eg to drive the music forward and create tension and drama)* and how it does this *(eg it is very rhythmic and often uses short note values, syncopation and triplets)*.

- Ask pupils if they can remember the bass ostinato from *Gladiator demo* and invite a pupil to demonstrate it using the word rhythm they learnt in lesson 1, activity 3 *(hurrying trailer one, two, sh)*.

- Divide the class into the same pairs as last lesson to revise their bass ostinati, taking into account to the comments they received at the end of last lesson and the notes they made on **Composing a bass ostinato** (printout 7).

- Combine pairs into larger groups. Each pair demonstrates their bass ostinato to the group and the group decides which ostinato best reflects the mood of the *Gladiator* trailer.

TEACHING TIP
As the bass ostinato is so fundamental to music of this genre, it is important that each group chooses one which is strong. If any groups are struggling, suggest they use the one from *Gladiator demo* (track 5) which they have already learned.

LESSON 2
BASS OSTINATO AND MELODY

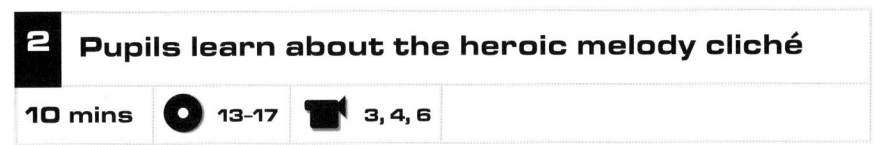

2 Pupils learn about the heroic melody cliché

10 mins   13–17   3, 4, 6

KEY WORDS

scale – an arrangement of specific notes played in order of pitch from the lowest to the highest (or vice versa).

- Explain that pupils will learn about the heroic melody cliché used in music for action film trailers.

- Watch video clips 3, 4 and 6 and ask pupils to identify which family of instruments play the melody in each *(brass instruments)*.

- Watch the video clips again and this time ask pupils to identify how the melody helps to capture the mood of the trailer in each clip *(eg the brass instruments sound triumphant; the melodies are loud and exciting)*.

- Listen to the melody and bass ostinato from *Gladiator demo* (track 13) and discuss how they fit together in this piece *(eg the melody begins after four repeats of the ostinato)*.

- Play the looped bass and untuned percussion ostinati from *Gladiator demo* (track 14) and demonstrate the following examples of heroic melodies in time with the bass ostinati (either on a tuned instrument or using your voice). Alternatively use tracks 15–17, observing:
  - how the melodies keep coming back to the note A;
  - how some use long note values and others use short, rhythmic notes;
  - how they are very repetitive and made up of short phrases.

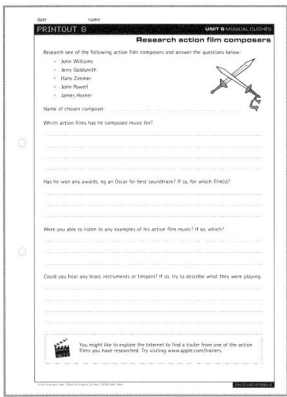

Printout 8: Research action film composers

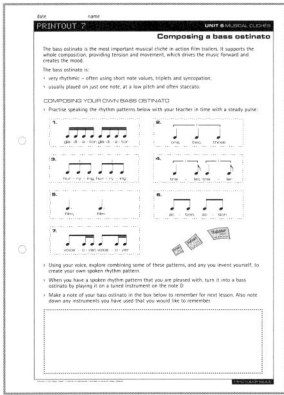

Printout 7: Composing a bass ostinato

- Explain the term **scale** and that *Gladiator demo* uses notes from the scale DEFGABCD.

LESSON 2
BASS OSTINATO AND MELODY

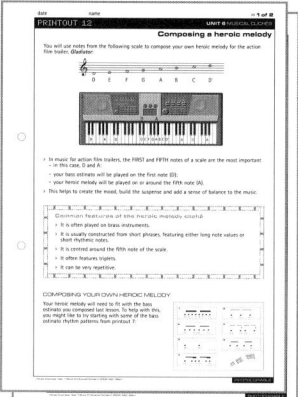

Printout 12: Composing a heroic melody (2 pages)

- Explain that in music for action film trailers, the first and fifth notes of the scale are the most important. For example, the bass ostinato in *Gladiator demo* is played on or around the first note of the scale (D) and the heroic melody around the fifth note (A).

3 Pupils begin composing a heroic melody to fit with their bass ostinato

KEYBOARD page 24   **ICT** page 25

15 mins

- Distribute copies of *Composing a heroic melody* (printout 12). Explain that:
  - pupils will work in their groups to begin to compose their own heroic melody ideas to go with the bass ostinato their group chose in activity 1;
  - their melody will use notes from the scale, DEFGABCD;
  - their melody should be centred around the note A;
  - they may use any of the rhythmic or melodic starting points given on printout 12.

- Explain that it is important for pupils to develop their melodic ideas alongside the bass ostinati they have composed. (One person in each group could play the bass ostinato while another experiments with melody and the rest of the group taps a steady pulse. Then pupils should swap over.)

- Each group should find a way to keep a note of their ideas using the space provided on printout 12 to remember for next lesson. They might like to invent a word rhythm to go with their melody to help them remember it.

EXTENSION ACTIVITY
Explain that the *Gladiator* trailer is 30 seconds long, so each group should work out how many times they need to repeat their bass ostinato to fit the length of the trailer as closely as possible. One pupil could time 30 seconds and count as another pupil repeats the ostinato.

TEACHING TIPS
Make sure pupils understand that the melody does not have to be finished in this lesson. Instead, pupils should concentrate on developing as many ideas as possible.

If you would prefer to give your pupils a choice of scales to use, the following work well, as they only use the white notes of a keyboard: EFGABCDE and ABCDEFGA.

To ensure the melody fits well with the bass ostinato, pupils might find it easier to use long rather than short note values.

4 Pupils perform their heroic melody ideas to the class

5 mins

- Invite as many groups as possible to perform their heroic melody ideas to the class. Ask the class to comment on:
  - how well the bass ostinato and heroic melody ideas fit together;
  - how well the ideas capture the mood and drama of the *Gladiator* trailer.

LESSON 2
BASS OSTINATO AND MELODY

Plenary
5 mins

- Ask pupils what they have learnt about action film trailer music this lesson *(eg the first and fifth notes of the scale are the most important; the heroic melody cliché sounds triumphant and is usually played on brass instruments)*.

- Pupils discuss how they might develop their heroic melody ideas next lesson *(eg they could experiment with different instruments or a different tempo)*.

Homework

- Pupils take home copies of **Key words** (printout 13) to learn for homework and **Composing a heroic melody** (printout 12) to develop more ideas for next lesson, if they have time.

- Remind pupils to bring in any instruments they need for their composition to the next lesson.

ASSESSMENT FOR LEARNING

- Who has remembered their bass ostinato from last lesson?
- Whose melodic ideas have a clear shape?
- Which groups are performing their ideas rhythmically?

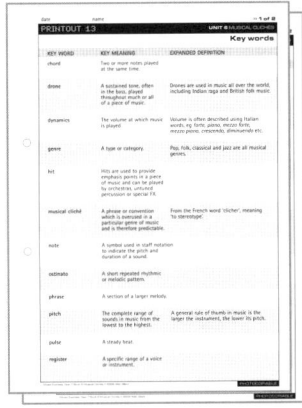

Printout 13: Key words
(2 pages)

KEYBOARD (see page 20)

1 Revise the bass ostinati composed last lesson

10 mins

- Revise the role of the bass ostinato in music for action film trailers, as described on page 20.

- Ask the pupils if they can remember the bass ostinato from *Gladiator demo*. Invite a pupil to demonstrate it using the word rhythm they learnt in lesson 1 or by playing it on a keyboard using the note D.

- Divide the class into the same pairs as last lesson to revise their bass ostinati taking into account to the comments they received at the end of last lesson and the notes they made on **Composing a bass ostinato – keyboard** (printout 9).

- Pupils select their chosen voice and then practise playing their bass ostinato at a steady tempo, making sure they play in time with each other.

- Combine pairs into larger groups. Each pair demonstrates their ostinato to the group and the group decides which ostinato best reflects the mood of the trailer.

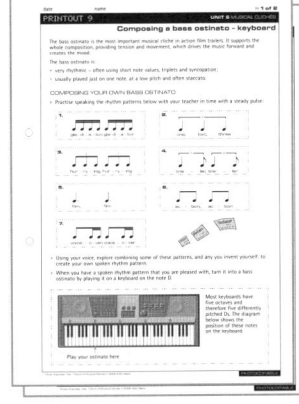

Printout 9: Composing a bass ostinato – keyboard
(2 pages)

TEACHING TIPS

If pupils have difficulty playing their ostinato at a steady tempo, suggest they use the metronome function on their keyboard to help them (eg 80bpm).

As the bass ostinato is so fundamental to music of this genre, it is important that each group chooses one which is strong. If any groups are struggling, suggest they use the one from *Gladiator demo* (track 5) which they have already learned.

RETURN TO ACTIVITY 2 (page 21)

LESSON 2
BASS OSTINATO AND MELODY

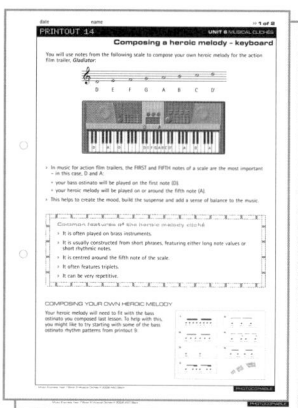

Printout 14: Composing a heroic melody – keyboard (2 pages)

KEYBOARD (see page 22)

3 **Pupils begin composing a heroic melody to fit with their bass ostinato**

15 mins • 12 • 14

- Distribute copies of *Composing a heroic melody – keyboard* (printout 14) and introduce the task as described on page 22.

- Pairs record their bass ostinato into the keyboard memory, if keyboards allow, and practise their melodic ideas alongside it. (Pupils should record several repeats of their bass ostinato, to allow them to practise their melodic ideas effectively.)

- Suggest pupils experiment with voices from the brass range for their heroic melody. They could try groups of instruments such as 'brass section' or 'sweet horns'. You might like to play track 12 (*Gladiator demo* composed with midi sounds) to demonstrate the kind of timbres the pupils might use.

- Once pairs have spent time coming up with ideas, they demonstrate them to their groups. Each group then decides which ideas best reflect the mood of the trailer.

- Each group should find a way to keep a note of their ideas in the space provided on printout 14 to remember for next lesson.

EXTENSION ACTIVITY
Explain that the *Gladiator* trailer is 30 seconds long, so each group should work out how many times they need to repeat their bass ostinato to fit the length of the trailer as closely as possible. One pupil could time 30 seconds and count as another pupil repeats the bass ostinato.

TEACHING TIPS
Make sure pupils understand that the heroic melody does not have to be finished in this lesson. Instead, pupils should concentrate on developing as many ideas as possible.

Fingering is suggested for the heroic melody starting points on printout 14, if required.

If keyboard models do not allow the bass ostinato to be recorded into the memory, suggest that pupils use the split voice function by selecting VOICE and trying out any of the numbers given. One pupil then tries out heroic melody ideas while another plays the bass ostinato. Encourage pupils to swap roles regularly.

« RETURN TO ACTIVITY 4 (page 22)

LESSON 2
BASS OSTINATO AND MELODY

ICT (see page 20)

1 Revise the bass ostinati composed last lesson

10 mins

- Revise the role of the bass ostinato in music for action film trailers, as described on page 20.

- Revise the bass ostinato from *Gladiator demo* by playing *gladiator.mid* in the sequencer and using the SOLO button to isolate the bass ostinato. Encourage pupils to follow the notes on the screen as they listen.

- The ICT group opens the bass ostinato they composed last lesson in the sequencer edit window. They listen to it and refine it, taking into account the comments they received at the end of last lesson and using *Composing a bass ostinato using a midi sequencer* (printout 10) to help them.

- Pupils use 'Repeating your bass ostinato' on printout 10 to help them repeat their bass ostinato to fill 30 seconds.

TEACHING TIP
As the bass ostinato is so fundamental to music of this genre it is important that each group chooses one which is strong. If any groups are struggling, suggest they use the one from *Gladiator demo* (track 5).

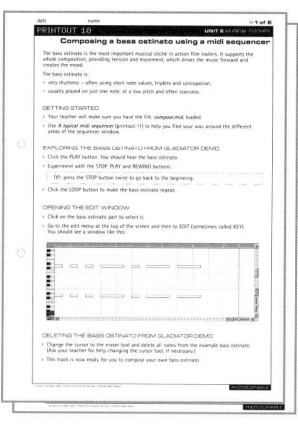

Printout 10: Composing a bass ostinato using a midi sequencer (2 pages)

RETURN TO ACTIVITY 2 (page 21)

ICT (see page 22)

3 Pupils begin composing a heroic melody to fit with their bass ostinato

15 mins

- For this activity, pupils will need a midi keyboard connected to their computer. Before the lesson, create a new track named 'melody', with the patch number configured to a brass sound, eg 62.

- Distribute copies of *Composing a heroic melody* (printout 12) and introduce the task as described on page 22.

- Pupils begin to to explore ideas for their heroic melody, rehearsing them on the keyboard and playing along with their bass ostinato as they work.

- Encourage pupils to record their ideas, using *Composing a heroic melody using a midi sequencer* (printout 15) to help them.

EXTENSION ACTIVITY
Once the group has recorded their ideas, they experiment with different timbres by changing the patch number of the melody track (57–64 are brass sounds). You could play track 12 (*Gladiator demo* composed with midi sounds) to demonstrate timbres the pupils could use.

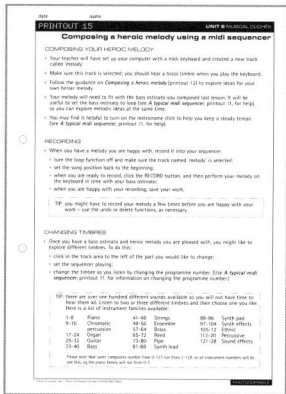

Printout 15: Composing a heroic melody using a midi sequencer

RETURN TO ACTIVITY 4 (page 22)

25

Lesson 3 — Adding a drone

OBJECTIVES

By the end of the lesson pupils should:

- understand the role of each instrumental part and its relationship to the others in their composition;
- understand the role of the drone cliché.

OUTCOMES

Pupils:

- continue to develop ideas for their heroic melody, and compose a suitable drone;
- perform their musical ideas in time with each other.

RESOURCES

AUDIO CD
Tracks 13–14, 18–19

CD-ROM
- Presentation
- Video clips 4–5
- Printouts 2, 11–12, 14–19
- Midi files (optional)
- Teacher information (optional)

INSTRUMENTS
- Untuned and tuned instruments (optional)
- Pupils bring in instruments from home (optional)
- Electronic keyboards (optional)

ICT
- Whiteboard or computer and data projector with sound
- Midi sequencer software and midi keyboard (optional)

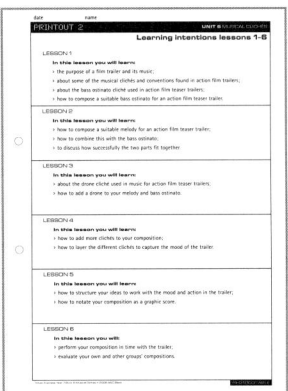

Printout 2: Learning intentions lessons 1–6

Focus
5 mins · 14 · Presentation

- Introduce the learning intentions for this lesson using the presentation on the CD-ROM or printout 2.

- Play the looped bass and percussion ostinati from *Gladiator demo* (track 14) and encourage pupils to clap along to the pulse. Then play or sing one of the examples below in time with the looped ostinati and select a pupil to sing a short answering phrase, starting on the note you finished on.

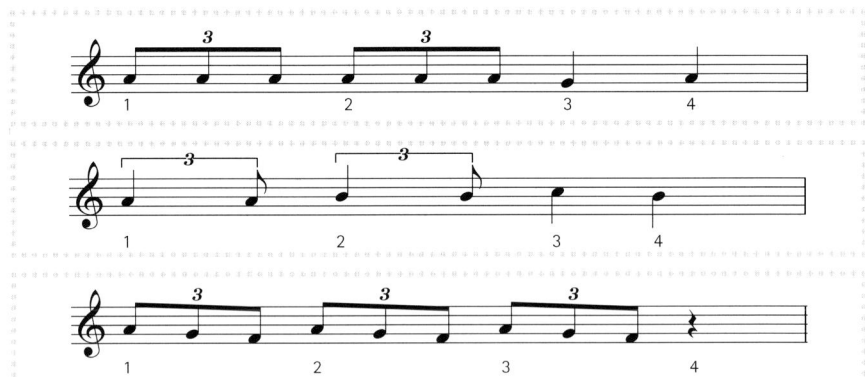

- Repeat the exercise as desired, choosing different pupils each time.

TEACHING TIPS

If pupils have difficulty creating a melodic answering phrase, encourage them to respond using spoken phrases instead, drawing on the spoken rhythm patterns learnt in lesson 1.

You may also like to develop your own starting phrases in addition to those given above.

1 Pupils are set their composition task
5 mins · 4 · 16 17 18

- Distribute copies of **Composition ideas bank** (printout 17), then display **Composing guidelines** (printout 18) and revise the composition brief, explaining that pupils will continue to work in groups to compose music to accompany the *Gladiator* teaser trailer.

- Watch the *Gladiator* trailer (video clip 4) and revise as a class the mood their composition needs to create *(eg it should create a sense of momentum and a feeling of suspense; it should be serious, dramatic and exciting)*.

LESSON 3
ADDING A DRONE

- Revise the two clichés the pupils have learnt so far – the bass ostinato and the heroic melody – and discuss how these clichés can help create this mood eg:
  - the bass ostinato is very rhythmic and its purpose is to drive the music forward;
  - the heroic melody adds drama and a sense of triumph; it is often played on brass instruments.

- Display the *Assessment criteria* (printout 16) and go through the level descriptions.

KEY WORDS

drone – a sustained tone, often in the bass, played throughout much or all of a piece of music.

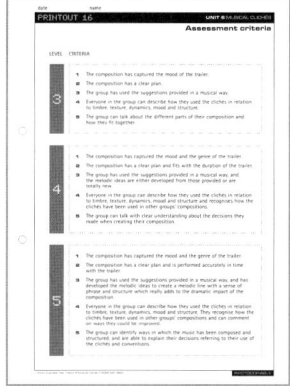

Printout 16: Assessment criteria

- Divide the class into their groups to review their bass ostinati and develop their heroic melody ideas further. Encourage each group to:
  - work out how many times their bass ostinato will need to be played to fill 30 seconds, if they haven't already done so;
  - revise and develop ideas for their heroic melody following the comments they received from the class last lesson and the notes they made on *Composing a heroic melody* (printout 12);
  - practise their heroic melody ideas and bass ostinato in time with each other;
  - keep a note of any ideas on *Composition ideas bank* (printout 17).

TEACHING TIP
You might like to allow groups to practise their bass ostinato alongside the *Gladiator* trailer (video clip 5) to help them fill 30 seconds. Alternatively, they could use a stopwatch to time 30 seconds. If pupils have difficulty fitting an exact number of repeats of their bass ostinato into 30 seconds, encourage them to get as close to 30 seconds as possible.

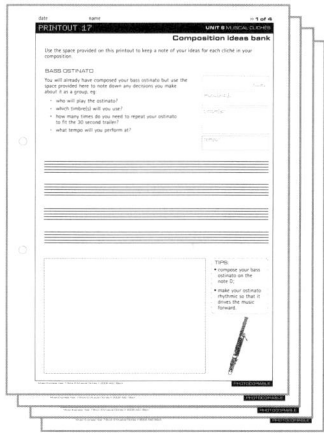

Printout 17: Composition ideas bank (4 pages)

- Listen to track 18. Explain that this is the bass ostinato and heroic melody from *Gladiator demo*, which they are already familiar with, but that a third layer has been added. Ask pupils to describe what they hear. *(A drone is present for the majority of the piece.)*

TEACHING TIP
If the pupils have difficulty picking out the drone, you might like to play track 13 (bass ostinato and heroic melody) as a comparison.

- Explain the term **drone**.

- Tell pupils that drones can be found in music from all over the world and that they are also one of the clichés often heard in music for action film trailers.

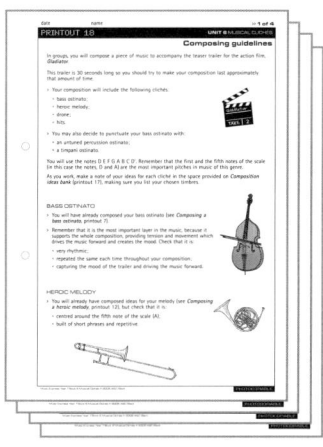

Printout 18: Composing guidelines (4 pages)

LESSON 3
ADDING A DRONE

KEY WORDS

texture – the number of performers in a piece.

tremolo – the fast repetition of a note, often by strings or percussion.

ASSESSMENT FOR LEARNING

- Who is using the new terminology when working in their groups?
- Which groups need additional support?
- Who has a clear perception of which timbres work best?
- Are the compositions beginning to convey the mood of the trailer?

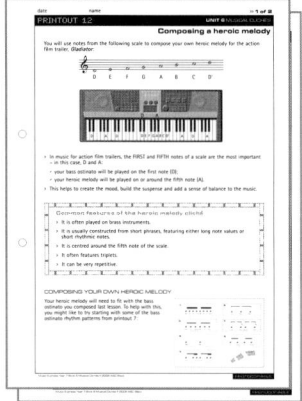

Printout 12: Composing a heroic melody (2 pages)

- Explain that the drone on track 18 is made up of two sustained notes: the first and fifth notes of the scale. Remind pupils that these are the most important notes of the scale.

- Demonstrate the drone by playing the extract below or listening to track 19.

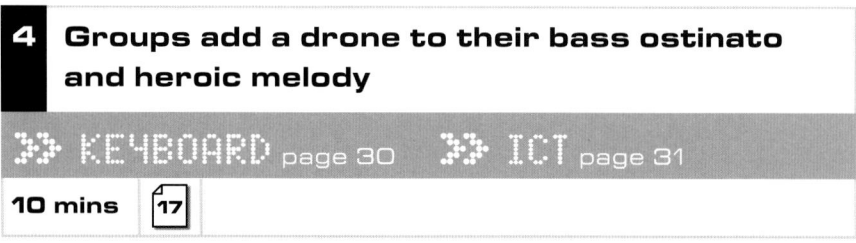

- Explain the term **texture**. Listen again to track 18 and ask pupils to describe the effect of the drone on the texture *(eg it thickens the texture; it fills in gaps in the texture and it creates a serious atmosphere).*

4 Groups add a drone to their bass ostinato and heroic melody

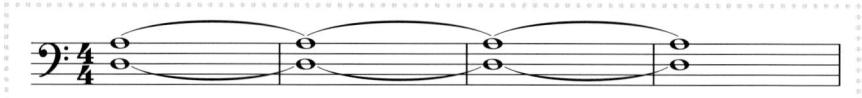

KEYBOARD page 30   **ICT** page 31

10 mins   17

- Pupils work in their groups to add a drone to their bass ostinato and heroic melody. Explain that their drone can either be on the note D alone, or on the notes D and A together.

- Pupils decide when to add their drone to their bass ostinato. They might like to introduce it at the beginning of their composition, or after a few repetitions of the bass ostinato.

- Encourage pupils to begin to think carefully about the best timbres for each of the clichés they have developed so far, for example:
  - the drone will need to be played on an instrument capable of sustaining notes for a long duration (eg strings, keyboard);
  - the bass ostinato will need to be played on a low-pitched instrument which is capable of playing short, rhythmic notes (eg 'cello, bassoon, tuba);
  - the heroic melody is usually played on a brass instrument (eg trumpet, horn, trombone).

- Pupils should make a note of the timbres they choose and any other ideas on *Composition ideas bank* (printout 17).

EXTENSION ACTIVITY

Pupils experiment with altering the volume of their drone, considering whether changing its volume during their composition could help build the music to a climax.

TEACHING TIPS

If no sustaining instruments are available, the drone may be played as a roll or **tremolo** on tuned percussion. It could also be played on another tuned instrument, breathing or restriking the keys where appropriate.

The pupils' compositions will work best with the clichés introduced later in this unit if they are restricted to using the note D or the notes D and A together for the drone.

LESSON 3
ADDING A DRONE

Plenary

5 mins

- Discuss with pupils the composition task they have been set and what they consider the challenges to be *(eg performing their clichés in time with each other; using the timbres they have available to create the intended mood, etc)*.

- Brainstorm any ideas the pupils have to help with this.

TEACHING TIP
If pupils don't have access to the suggested instruments, the teacher will need to help find alternatives. If this is the case, make sure pupils realise that they will be assessed on the way they use the clichés in their composition, not on the actual instrumentation.

Homework

- Ask pupils to find out which musical genres feature drones most prominently and which instruments are commonly associated with drones.

- Remind pupils to bring in any instruments from home that they need for the next lesson.

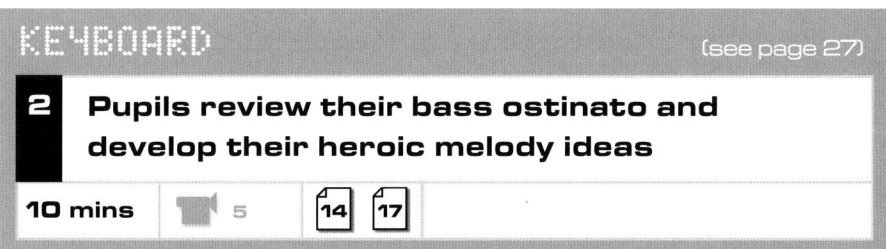

KEYBOARD   (see page 27)

2 Pupils review their bass ostinato and develop their heroic melody ideas

10 mins   5   14   17

- Divide the class into their groups to revise their bass ostinati and develop their heroic melody ideas further. Encourage each group to:

  • work out how many times their bass ostinato will need to be played to fill 30 seconds, if they haven't already done so, and record this into the keyboard memory, if keyboards allow;
  • revise and develop ideas for their heroic melody following the comments they received from the class last lesson and the notes they made on *Composing a heroic melody – keyboard* (printout 14);
  • practise their heroic melody ideas and bass ostinato in time with each other;
  • keep a note of any ideas on *Composition ideas bank* (printout 17).

TEACHING TIP
You might like to allow groups to practise their bass ostinato alongside the *Gladiator* trailer (video clip 5) to help them fill 30 seconds. Alternatively, they could use a stopwatch to time 30 seconds. If pupils have difficulty fitting an exact number of repeats of their bass ostinato into 30 seconds, encourage them to get as close to 30 seconds as possible.

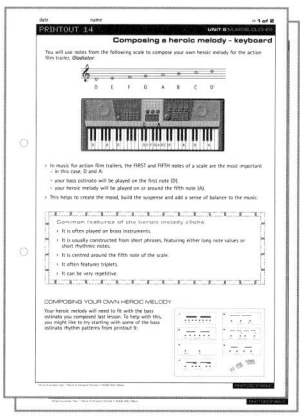

Printout 14: Composing a heroic melody – keyboard (2 pages)

« RETURN TO ACTIVITY 3   (page 27)

LESSON 3
ADDING A DRONE

KEY WORDS

register – a specific range of a voice or instrument.

Printout 15: Composing a heroic melody using a midi sequencer

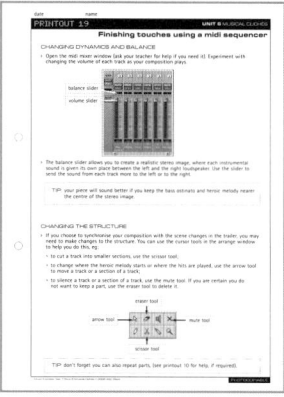

Printout 19: Finishing touches using a midi sequencer

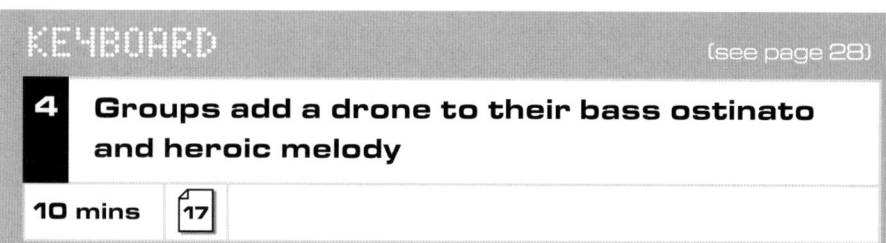

- Introduce the task as described on page 28.

- Define the term **register.** Encourage pupils to consider the most suitable register and voice for their drone, experimenting with sounds from the symphony orchestra as well as more exotic timbres and taking into account how effective these instruments sound in the register they have chosen.

- Pupils decide when to add their drone to their bass ostinato. They might like to introduce it at the beginning, or after a few repetitions of the bass ostinato.

- Pupils should make a note of their ideas on *Composition ideas bank* (printout 17).

EXTENSION ACTIVITY

Pupils experiment with altering the volume of their drone, considering whether changing its volume during their composition could help build the music to a climax.

RETURN TO PLENARY (page 29)

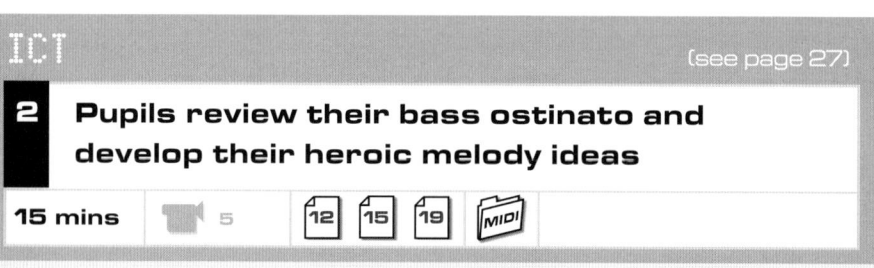

- Pupils open their composition in the sequencer and listen to their bass ostinato and heroic melody together. They revise and develop them, taking into account the comments they received last lesson.

EXTENSION ACTIVITY

Show pupils how tension is created in *gladiator.mid* by adding a melody voice one octave higher towards the climax of the composition:

- in the arrange window, create a new track for the pupils with the same patch number as the melody track. Copy the melody to the new track and transpose the copy up one octave. (Consult your sequencer manual for help, if necessary.)

- pupils decide where the higher voice should occur in their composition. They use the scissor tool to cut the track at that point and the eraser tool to delete the part not needed, using *Finishing touches using a midi sequencer* (printout 19) to help them.

TEACHING TIPS

Allow groups to listen to their work alongside the *Gladiator* trailer (video clip 5), if possible, to assess whether their composition is beginning to convey the mood of the trailer.

Make sure pupils have a copy of *Composing a heroic melody* (printout 12) and *Composing a heroic melody using a midi sequencer* (printout 15) to hand as they work.

RETURN TO ACTIVITY 3 (page 27)

LESSON 3
ADDING A DRONE

ICT (see page 28)

4 Groups add a drone to their bass ostinato and heroic melody

10 mins [11] [MIDI]

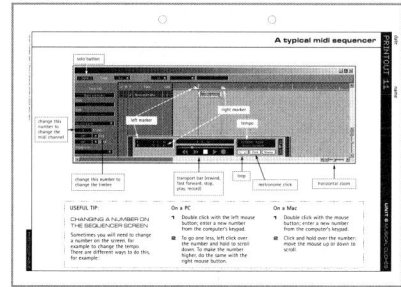

Printout 11: A typical midi sequencer

- Before the lesson, open the file *compose.mid* and create a new track named 'drone', with the patch number configured to a suitable sound, eg 90.

- Introduce the task as described on page 28.

- Pupils rehearse their drone ideas on the midi keyboard, listening to and playing along with their bass ostinato and heroic melody as they work.

- Pupils record their drone when they are happy with it and then experiment with suitable timbres for the three clichés they have composed so far, as described on page 28.

TEACHING TIPS

The pupils' compositions will work best with the clichés introduced later in this unit if they are restricted to using the note D or the notes D and A together for the drone.

If the pupils find it hard to choose timbres, limit their choice to the following patch numbers:

- bass ostinato: 48, 46, 39;
- melody: 62, 63, 82, 85;
- drone: 90, 92, 96, 88, 86.

Pupils might find it useful to refer to *A typical midi sequencer* (printout 11) for help changing patch numbers.

« RETURN TO PLENARY (page 29)

Lesson 4 — Hits and percussion

OBJECTIVES
By the end of the lesson pupils should:
- be confident about performing their musical ideas;
- understand the role of the hits cliché and percussion clichés.

OUTCOMES
Pupils:
- introduce hits and percussion into their composition;
- perform and discuss their work in progress.

RESOURCES

AUDIO CD
Track 7

CD-ROM
- Presentation
- Video clips 4–6
- Printouts 2, 10–11, 15–18
- Midi files (optional)
- Teacher information (optional)

INSTRUMENTS
- Untuned and tuned instruments (optional)
- Pupils bring in instruments from home (optional)
- Timpani tuned to D and A (optional)
- Electronic keyboards (optional)

ICT
- Whiteboard or computer and data projector with sound
- Midi sequencer software and midi keyboard (optional)
- Recording equipment (optional)

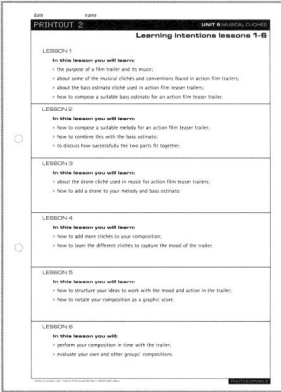

Printout 2: Learning intentions lessons 1–6

Focus — 5 mins — 2, 18 — Presentation

- Display **Composing guidelines** (printout 18) and revise the composition brief. Explain that in this lesson pupils will continue to develop the clichés they have composed so far *(bass ostinato, heroic melody and drone)* and explore adding hits and percussion ostinati to their composition.

- Discuss the learning intentions for this lesson using the presentation on the CD-ROM or printout 2.

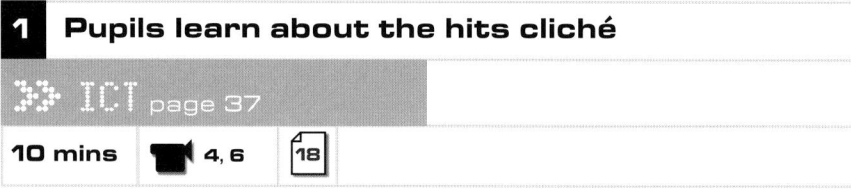

1 Pupils learn about the hits cliché

ICT page 37

10 mins — 4, 6 — 18

- Explain the term **hit** and then go through the hits cliché as used in music for action film trailers, demonstrating the examples given on printout 18.

- Watch the *Gladiator* trailer with the original soundtrack (video clip 4) and with *Gladiator demo* (video clip 6) twice each, so that the music becomes familiar. Then watch each clip again and ask pupils to identify the hits and try to clap in time with them when they occur.

- Discuss:
  - how the hits are unpredictable and therefore difficult to clap in time with;
  - how the hits don't always fall on the beat;
  - how the hits sometimes coincide with scene changes (eg in the original *Gladiator* trailer), but they are still not easy to predict;
  - the role of the hits *(eg just as the trailer contains visual shocks and surprises, the hits add spikes of dramatic tension which help bring the music to a climax)*.

TEACHING TIP
You might like to explain that hits don't always correspond to scene changes in action film trailers but that they can do if desired.

LESSON 4
HITS AND PERCUSSION

2 Groups revise their work from last lesson and explore adding hits to their composition

KEYBOARD page 35 **ICT** page 38

10 mins 🎥 5 📄 16 17 18

- In their groups, pupils revise the work they have done so far on their bass ostinato, heroic melody and drone, using the notes they made on *Composition ideas bank* (printout 17), and then explore adding hits to the texture.

- Remind pupils to think carefully about suitable timbres for each cliché and listen to how well the clichés combine to create the overall mood.

- Encourage pupils to consider the role of the hits in their composition, (eg they might help build the music to a climax by becoming more frequent towards the end, or they might coincide with scene changes in the *Gladiator* trailer).

TEACHING TIPS

Ensure pupils have copies of *Assessment criteria* (printout 16) and *Composing guidelines* (printout 18) to hand as they work. They should also continue to make a note of their ideas on *Composition ideas bank* (printout 17).

Encourage pupils to continue adjusting their ideas to get the best effects possible. There will be time next lesson to settle on their final ideas and rehearse them.

If pupils are struggling to find notes that work for their hits, suggest they try out the options on printout 18.

It may be useful to allow different groups time to work with the trailer (video clip 5) to help them assess whether their music is successfully capturing the mood of the trailer. A 5–4–3–2–1 countdown is provided so they know when to start.

KEY WORDS

hit – hits are used to provide emphasis points in a piece of music and can be played by orchestras, untuned percussion or special FX.

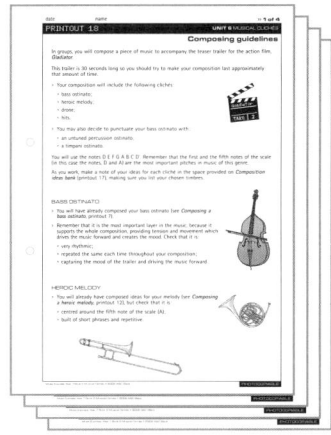

Printout 18: Composing guidelines (4 pages)

3 Pupils learn about the timpani and untuned percussion clichés

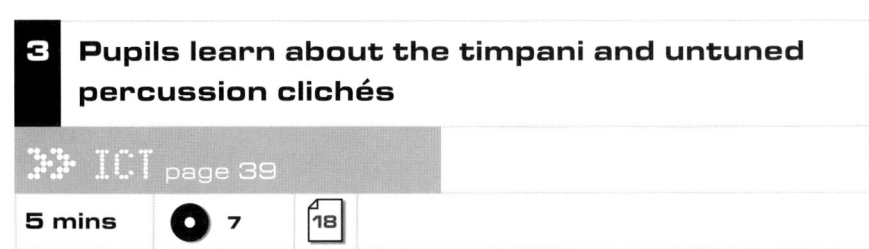

ICT page 39

5 mins 💿 7 📄 18

- Display the section entitled 'Punctuating your bass ostinato with percussion' on *Composing guidelines* (printout 18) and explain that pupils also have the option of adding a timpani and/or untuned percussion ostinato to their composition.

- Demonstrate the examples on printout 18 on any untuned percussion and/or timpani you have available or by asking pupils to clap the rhythms. Then listen to track 7 (bass, timpani and percussion ostinati) and discuss how the three ostinati fit together, noting in particular how:
  • the untuned percussion and timpani ostinati help to emphasise certain notes of the bass ostinato;
  • the combined ostinati help to drive the bass ostinato forward.

TEACHING TIP

If no timpani and/or untuned percussion are available, pupils could use an appropriate voice on an electronic keyboard or body percussion for each ostinato respectively.

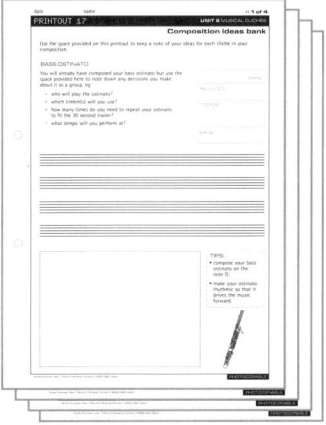

Printout 17: Composition ideas bank (4 pages)

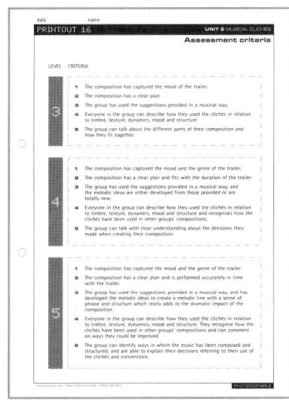

Printout 16: Assessment criteria

LESSON 4
HITS AND PERCUSSION

ASSESSMENT FOR LEARNING

- Do the different clichés fit well together?
- Are the groups successfully overcoming problems with accuracy and timing?

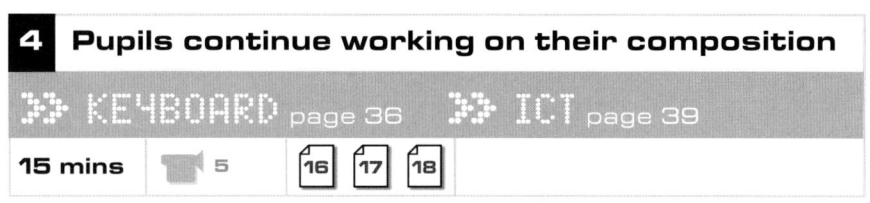

4 Pupils continue working on their composition

>> KEYBOARD page 36   >> ICT page 39

15 mins   5   16 17 18

- Pupils continue working in their groups to develop ideas for their composition, exploring the suggestions on *Composing guidelines* (printout 18) and rehearsing their ideas as they work. They should consider:
  - whether they will add untuned percussion and/or timpani ostinati to their music and if so, what untuned percussion they will use;
  - how these extra ostinati will fit with their bass ostinato;
  - when these ostinati will enter;
  - who will play each part.

- Explain that pupils do not need to use all the clichés they have learnt to make their composition successful. If they do not feel confident about the clichés they have composed so far *(bass ostinato, melody, drone and hits)*, they should use this time to finish these, rather than adding further clichés to their work.

- Pupils should keep a note of their chosen timbres and any other ideas or elements that need practising on *Composition ideas bank* (printout 17).

EXTENSION ACTIVITY

If possible, groups should record their work in progress and listen back to assess whether their music is successfully capturing the mood of the trailer.

TEACHING TIPS

Ensure pupils have a copy of *Assessment criteria* (printout 16) to hand as they work.

It may be useful to allow different groups time to work with the trailer (video clip 5) to help them assess whether their music is successfully capturing the mood of the trailer. A *5–4–3–2–1* countdown is provided so they know when to start.

If resources are limited, pupils should swap instruments regularly. If no timpani and/or untuned percussion are available, pupils could use an appropriate voice on an electronic keyboard, body percussion, or their own voices for each ostinato.

Those adding untuned percussion or timpani ostinati to their composition will find it helpful to practise these parts with the bass ostinato until they are well established before trying them with the other clichés.

Plenary
5 mins

- Invite as many groups as possible to demonstrate their work in progress. They may choose to demonstrate all or just a couple of clichés together, depending on what they would like feedback on.

- Ask the class to comment on:
  - how well the musical ideas capture the mood and drama of the *Gladiator* trailer;
  - whether any parts are particularly effective;
  - how the musical ideas could be improved.

LESSON 4
HITS AND PERCUSSION

Homework

- Encourage pupils to watch a couple of trailers for a different genre of film, (eg romantic comedy, thriller, or family comedy) and ask them to think about whether these trailers use the same musical clichés as action film trailers and if not, whether they can identify any other clichés.

- Remind pupils to bring in any instruments they need from home to the next lesson.

TEACHING TIP
Pupils could look for trailers in the bonus material of any DVDs they have at home or on the Internet (eg www.apple.com/trailers). This website was suitable at the time of publication.

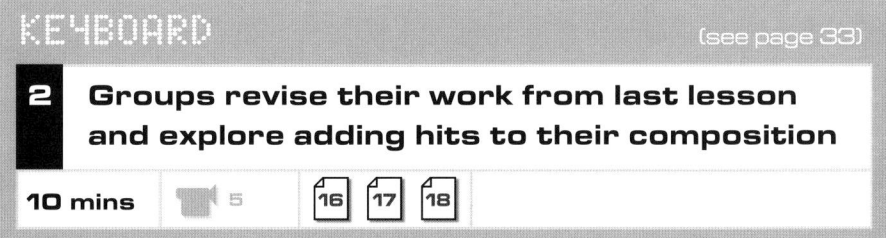

KEYBOARD (see page 33)

2 Groups revise their work from last lesson and explore adding hits to their composition

10 mins　📹 5　　[16] [17] [18]

- In their composition groups, pupils revise the work they have done so far on their bass ostinato, heroic melody and drone, using the notes they made on *Composition ideas bank* (printout 17), and then explore adding hits to the texture.

- Pupils could use this time to save their work to floppy disk or to record their work into the keyboard memory, if keyboards allow.

- Encourage pupils to:
  - consider the role of the hits in their composition, (eg they might help build the music to a climax by becoming more frequent towards the end, or they might coincide with scene changes in the *Gladiator* trailer);
  - experiment with timbres for their hits. Suggest they select VOICE and choose 'orchestral hit' (usually located under 'strings') and/or try out some sounds on synthesised pads, especially sounds which are dramatic, loud and staccato;
  - keep a note of their ideas on printout 17.

TEACHING TIPS
Ensure pupils have a copy of *Assessment criteria* (printout 16) and *Composing guidelines* (printout 18) to hand as they work.

Encourage groups to continue adjusting their ideas to get the best effects possible. There will be time next lesson to settle on their final ideas and rehearse them.

It may be useful to allow different groups time to work with the trailer (video clip 5) to help them assess whether their music is successfully capturing the mood of the trailer. A *5–4–3–2–1* countdown is provided so they know when to start.

 **TO ACTIVITY 3**　　　　(page 33)

LESSON 4
HITS AND PERCUSSION

KEYBOARD (see page 34)

4 Pupils continue working on their composition

15 mins | 5 | 16 17 18

- Pupils continue working in their groups to develop ideas for their composition, exploring the suggestions on *Composing guidelines* (printout 18) and rehearsing their ideas as they work. They should consider:
  - whether they will add untuned percussion and/or timpani ostinati to their music and if so, what untuned percussion they will use;
  - how these extra ostinati will fit with their bass ostinato;
  - when these ostinati will enter;
  - who will play each part and who will operate the volume control.

- Explain that pupils do not need to use all the clichés they have learnt to make their composition successful. If they do not feel confident about the clichés they have composed so far *(bass ostinato, melody, drone and hits)*, they should use this time to finish these, rather than adding further clichés to their work.

- Pupils should keep a note of their ideas and any elements that need practising on *Composition ideas bank* (printout 17).

EXTENSION ACTIVITY

For those pupils producing the composition entirely at the keyboard, introduce the TRANSPOSE function (usually located to the right of the display screen). One musical cliché used in action film trailers is to move the entire composition up a tone (+2 on the numeric keypad). This usually happens towards the end of the music to heighten tension and dramatic effect. (To transpose on the keyboard, press the TRANSPOSE button and use +/– on the keyboard.)

TEACHING TIPS

Ensure pupils have a copy of *Assessment criteria* (printout 16) to hand as they work.

It may be useful to allow different groups time to work with the trailer (video clip 5) to help them assess whether their music is successfully capturing the mood of the trailer. A *5–4–3–2–1* countdown is provided so they know when to start.

« RETURN TO PLENARY (page 34)

LESSON 4
HITS AND PERCUSSION

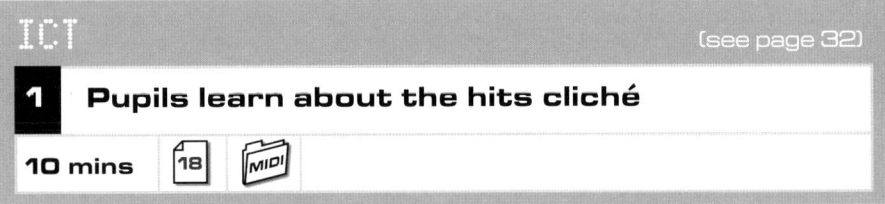

ICT (see page 32)

1 Pupils learn about the hits cliché

10 mins

- Explain the term **hit** and then go through the hits cliché as used in music for action film trailers, demonstrating the examples given on printout 18.

- Play the file *gladiator.mid* in the sequencer, asking the pupils to concentrate on listening to the hits and to watch the notes as they scroll by.

- Open the track named 'hits' in the edit window and play the file again. Use the SOLO button to demonstrate how the hits sound on their own.

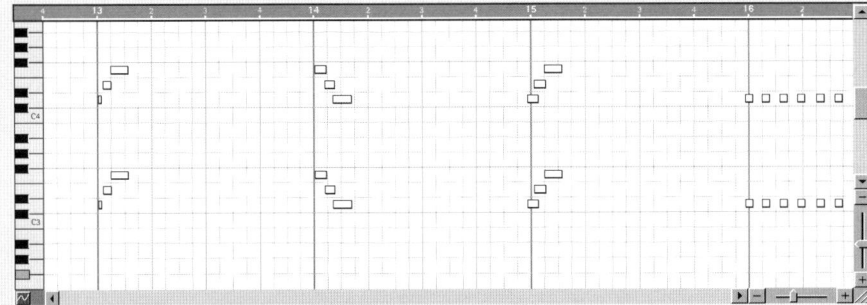

- Ask the class what they notice about the hits from watching the sequencer, eg:
  - they are more spread out at the beginning;
  - they start to double an octave apart towards the middle;
  - they first appear as clusters of notes (DEF / FED) but at the end they repeat on one note, doubled at the octave (D);
  - they do not always fall on the beat.

- Discuss the role of the hits *(eg just as the trailer contains visual shocks and surprises, the hits add spikes of dramatic tension which help bring the music to a climax).*

- Explain that the hits don't always correspond to changes of scene in action film trailers but that they can do if desired.

 **RETURN TO ACTIVITY 2** (page 33)

LESSON 4
HITS AND PERCUSSION

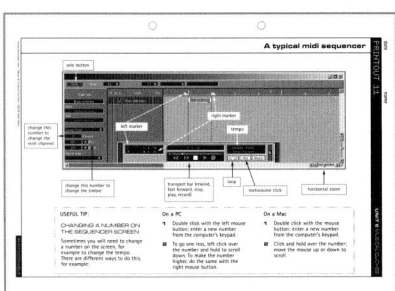

Printout 11: A typical midi sequencer

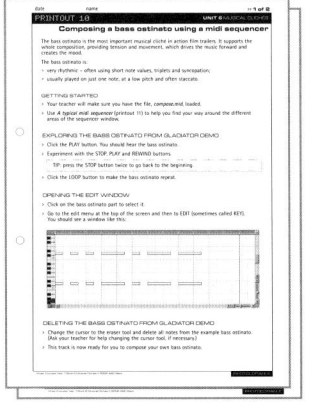

Printout 10: Composing a bass ostinato using a midi sequencer (2 pages)

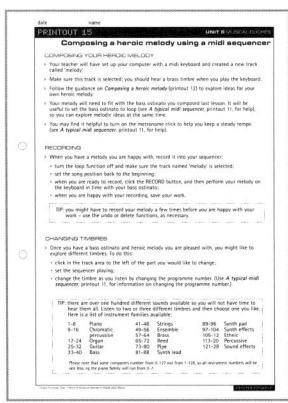

Printout 15: Composing a heroic melody using a midi sequencer

ICT
(see page 33)

2 Groups revise their work from last lesson and explore adding hits to their composition

10 mins | 10 | 11 | 15 | 16 | 18 | MIDI

- Before the lesson, open the pupils' compositions and create three new tracks named 'hits', 'timpani' and 'percussion'. Set the patch number for the hits track to 56, and the timpani track to 49. Configure the percussion track to midi channel 10. See *A typical midi sequencer* (printout 11) for help.

- Pupils revise the work they have done so far and explore adding hits to the texture. Tell the group they can choose to record their hits:
  - in real time using the RECORD button and midi keyboard, working in the same way as when they added their melody track in lesson 2.
  - or in step time in the edit window, using the mouse and working in the same way as when they created their bass ostinato in lesson 1.

EXTENSION ACTIVITY
Encourage pupils to experiment with doubling the hits an octave higher towards the end, as they did for the heroic melody in lesson 3 activity 2 (see page 30).

TEACHING TIPS
Ensure pupils have copies of *Composing a bass ostinato using a midi sequencer* (printout 10), *Composing a heroic melody using a midi sequencer* (printout 15), *Assessment criteria* (printout 16) and *Composing guidelines* (printout 18) to hand as they work.

Encourage groups to continue adjusting their ideas to get the best effects possible. There will be time next lesson to settle on their final ideas and rehearse them.

If pupils are struggling to find notes that work for their hits, they might like to try the suggestions on *Composing guidelines* (printout 18).

Remind pupils to save their work.

◄◄ RETURN TO ACTIVITY 3 (page 33)

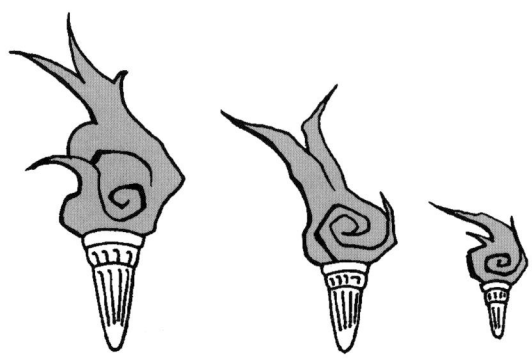

LESSON 4
HITS AND PERCUSSION

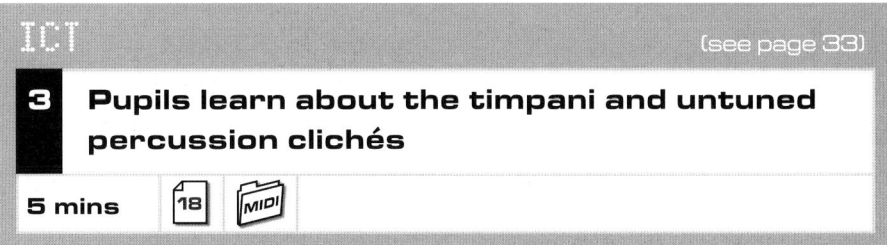

ICT (see page 33)

3 Pupils learn about the timpani and untuned percussion clichés

5 mins

- Display the section entitled 'Punctuating your bass ostinato with percussion' on *Composing guidelines* (printout 18).

- Open *gladiator.mid* in the edit window and demonstrate the untuned percussion and timpani ostinati to the class by soloing the tracks. Ask the class to listen carefully and describe what they notice about the percussion, eg:
  - the instruments used are timpani, cymbal, snare and bass drum;
  - the snare and bass drum patterns repeat throughout the composition;
  - the cymbal hits occur nearer the end of the piece, on the first beat of the bar;
  - the timpani play two notes (D and A).

RETURN TO ACTIVITY 4 (page 34)

ICT (see page 34)

4 Pupils continue working on their composition

15 mins

- Pupils punctuate their bass ostinato with percussion and timpani, using real time or step time input (see activity 2). Tell pupils that the timpani will have its own track, and that all the other percussion sounds can be recorded onto the percussion track.

TEACHING TIPS

Pupils will discover that there are many different untuned percussion sounds available as they play each note across the midi keyboard. You may need to show them which keys play the bass drum, snare and cymbal sounds:

- bass drum – C1;
- snare drum – D2;
- cymbal – C#2.

If pupils are using step time input, you may need to show them where to place the notes, using the keyboard guide to the left of the edit window.

It may be useful to allow different groups time to work with the trailer (video clip 5) to help them assess whether their music is successfully capturing the mood of the trailer. A 5–4–3–2–1 countdown is provided so they know when to start.

Ensure pupils have copies of *Composing a bass ostinato using a midi sequencer* (printout 10), *Composing a heroic melody using a midi sequencer* (printout 15) and *Composing guidelines* (printout 18) to hand as they work.

Remind pupils to save their work.

RETURN TO PLENARY (page 34)

Lesson 5 — Completing the structure

OBJECTIVES
By the end of the lesson pupils should:
- understand how to structure their ideas;
- understand the purpose of writing down a musical structure.

OUTCOMES
Pupils:
- are able to structure their music to fit the mood of the trailer;
- are able to make a simple score of their composition.

RESOURCES

AUDIO CD
Track 4

CD-ROM
- Presentation
- Video clips 4–5
- Printouts 2, 16–22
- Teacher information (optional)
- Midi files (optional)

INSTRUMENTS
- Untuned and tuned instruments (optional)
- Pupils bring in instruments from home (optional)
- Timpani tuned to D and A (optional)
- Electronic keyboards (optional)

ICT
- Whiteboard or computer and data projector with sound
- Midi sequencer software (optional)

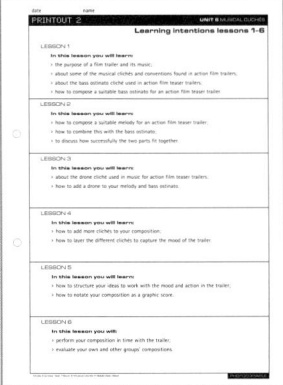

Printout 2: Learning intentions lessons 1–6

Focus
5 mins | 2 | **Presentation**

- Invite pupils to discuss the film trailers they watched for homework, stating:
  - whether any genres of trailer used the clichés they have encountered in action film trailers *(eg they may have found that thriller film trailers used the drone and heroic melody clichés)*;
  - whether they recognised any clichés in trailers of a different genre *(eg romantic comedies often use feel-good pop songs as trailer music)*.
- Discuss the learning intentions for this lesson using the presentation on the CD-ROM or printout 2.

1 Pupils revise their composition

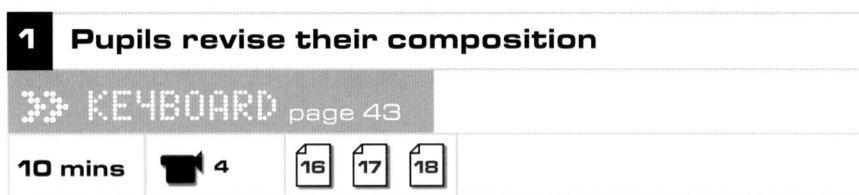

KEYBOARD page 43

10 mins | 4 | 16 | 17 | 18

- Watch the *Gladiator* teaser trailer with its original music (video clip 4) and revise the mood the pupils are trying to create in their composition.
- In their groups, pupils revise their composition so far, making sure they have:
  - a clear record of the instruments selected for the different clichés;
  - revised each cliché separately and rehearsed all the parts together;
  - made a note of things still to be decided or practised.

TEACHING TIP
Make sure each group has copies of *Assessment criteria* (printout 16), *Composition ideas bank* (printout 17) and *Composing guidelines* (printout 18) to hand as they work.

LESSON 5
COMPLETING THE STRUCTURE

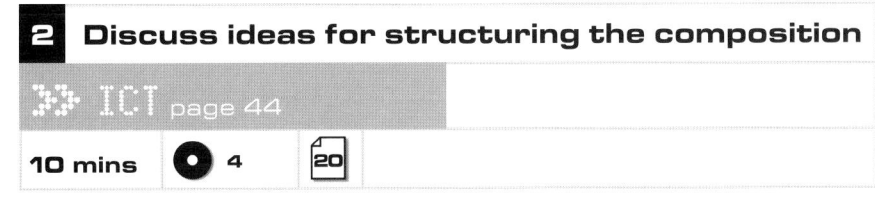

2 Discuss ideas for structuring the composition

ICT page 44

10 mins • 4 • 20

- Distribute copies of *Example composition plan* (printout 20). Explain the term **score** and play *Gladiator demo* (track 4), asking pupils to follow the graphic score as they listen to the music.

- Listen to track 4 again and this time ask pupils to describe the structure of the piece, with reference to printout 20 eg:
  - the piece starts with the bass ostinato alone;
  - the timpani and percussion ostinati enter with the drone;
  - the heroic melody joins in after four repetitions of the bass ostinato;
  - hits appear later, increasing in frequency as the music builds to a climax;
  - all parts play together in unison at the climax.

- Discuss how a graphic score could help pupils structure their own music eg:
  - it is a useful record of ideas to remember for next lesson;
  - it shows time passing and scene changes in the trailer, which could help pupils make effective structural decisions;
  - the score shows how the piece evolves and the grey shaded areas show when each player begins and ends.

3 Groups develop the structure of their composition

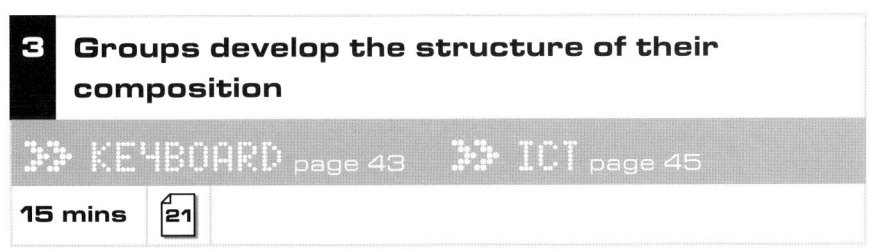

KEYBOARD page 43   **ICT** page 45

15 mins • 21

- Pupils work in their groups to revise the structure of their composition, (eg when the parts will enter, when the hits will be played etc), starting to fill in their ideas on *Composition plan* (printout 21) as they work.

- Pupils then consider:
  - whether the dynamics will build through the addition of extra parts, or whether they will build within each part as well;
  - whether they should appoint one person in charge of conducting or directing the group, or whether they will take their cues from the trailer;
  - how they might try to make their music fit approximately 30 seconds, if they haven't already done so, eg by sustaining the final note, or finishing with a series of hits.

TEACHING TIPS

Encourage pupils to keep modifying their ideas to get the best effects possible. There will be time in the next activity to finish their graphic score.

When groups are practising with the trailer, they should be aiming to make their piece last 30 seconds, but remind them that they will be assessed on how they use the clichés in their composition, not on the length of their composition.

KEY WORDS

score – a printed or sometimes handwritten depiction of a musical work.

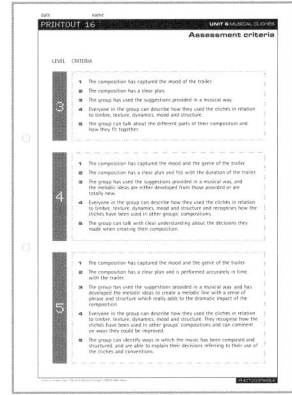

Printout 16: Assessment criteria

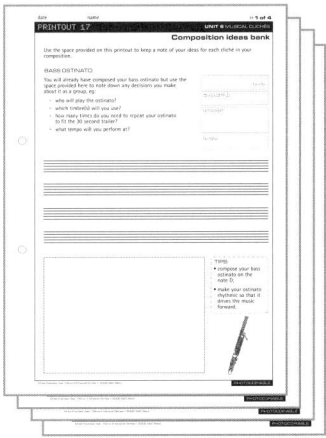

Printout 17: Composition ideas bank (4 pages)

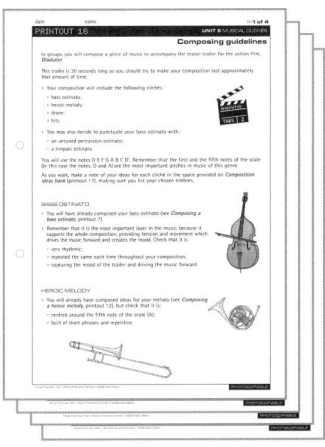

Printout 18: Composing guidelines (4 pages)

LESSON 5
COMPLETING THE STRUCTURE

ASSESSMENT FOR LEARNING

- Who has drawn up an effective composition plan?
- Who is suggesting improvements?
- Which compositions are beginning to communicate the mood of the trailer?

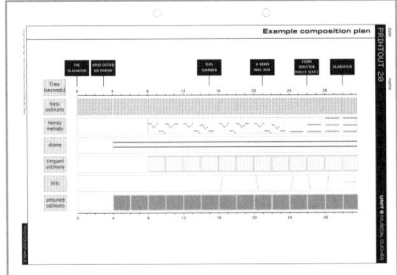

Printout 20: Example composition plan

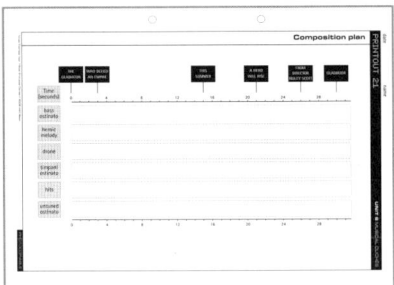

Printout 21: Composition plan

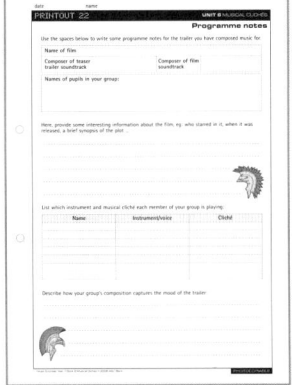

Printout 22: Programme notes

- Display **Assessment criteria** (printout 16). Revise the level descriptions and emphasise the importance of pupils' compositions having a clear structure.

- Each group then finishes their **Composition plan** (printout 21), making sure it is clear when each part begins and ends.

EXTENSION ACTIVITY
If possible, allow groups to practise their composition in time with the *Gladiator* trailer (video clip 5) using their composition plan. A 5–4–3–2–1 countdown is provided at the start of the trailer so they know when to start.

- Display **Example composition plan** (printout 20) and revise why writing down music is helpful *(eg it is a useful record of ideas to remember for next lesson; it shows how the piece evolves and when each player begins and ends)*.

- Ask pupils why a score is sometimes more helpful than writing down separate parts *(eg it is easier to see when different parts come in and to see how the texture changes during a piece of music)*.

Homework

- Ask pupils to write programme notes for the *Gladiator* teaser trailer accompanied by their group's composition, as if for a concert, using **Programme notes** (printout 22).

- Remind pupils to bring in any instruments from home to the next lesson that they need for their composition.

LESSON 5
COMPLETING THE STRUCTURE

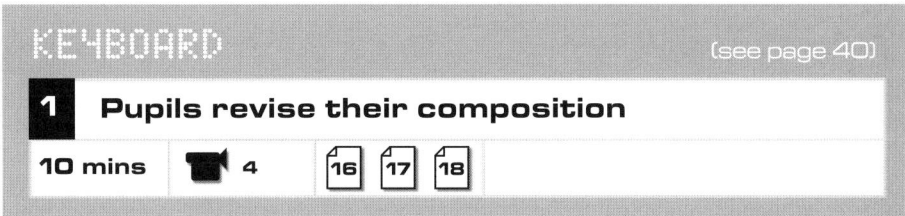

KEYBOARD (see page 40)

1 **Pupils revise their composition**

10 mins · 4 · 16 17 18

- Watch the *Gladiator* trailer with its original music (video clip 4) to revise the mood the pupils are trying to create in their composition.

- In their groups, pupils revise their composition so far, making sure they have:
  - a clear record of the voices selected for the different clichés;
  - revised each cliché separately and rehearsed all the parts together;
  - decided which ideas will be pre-recorded into the keyboard memory or disk (if keyboards allow) and which will be performed live;
  - decided in which register to play each cliché, considering not only what will create the best effect, but also what will be most practical to play;
  - made a note of things still to be decided or practised.

TEACHING TIP
Make sure each group has copies of *Assessment criteria* (printout 16), *Composition ideas bank* (printout 17) and *Composing guidelines* (printout 18) to hand as they work.

RETURN TO ACTIVITY 2 (page 41)

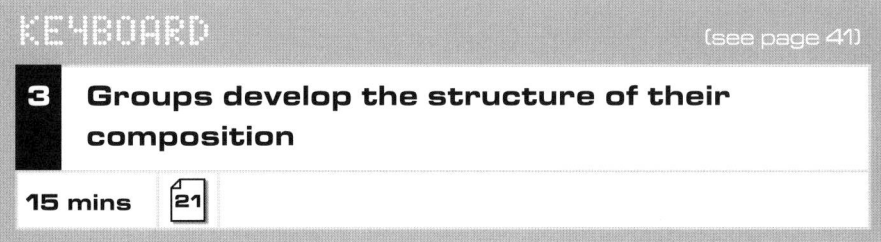

KEYBOARD (see page 41)

3 **Groups develop the structure of their composition**

15 mins · 21

- Pupils work in their groups to revise the structure of their composition, (eg when the parts will enter, when the hits will be played etc) and start to fill in their ideas on *Composition plan* (printout 21) as they work.

- Pupils then consider:
  - whether the dynamics will build through the addition of extra parts, or whether they will build within each part as well;
  - whether they should appoint one person in charge of conducting or directing the group, or whether they will take their cues from the trailer;
  - how they might try to make their music last approximately 30 seconds, if they haven't already done so, eg by altering the tempo, sustaining the final note, slowing down at the end or finishing with a series of hits.

TEACHING TIP
Each part may be recorded on a separate track, if keyboards allow, and then muted accordingly, so that pupils can test structural ideas by exploring different combinations of clichés.

RETURN TO ACTIVITY 4 (page 42)

LESSON 5
COMPLETING THE STRUCTURE

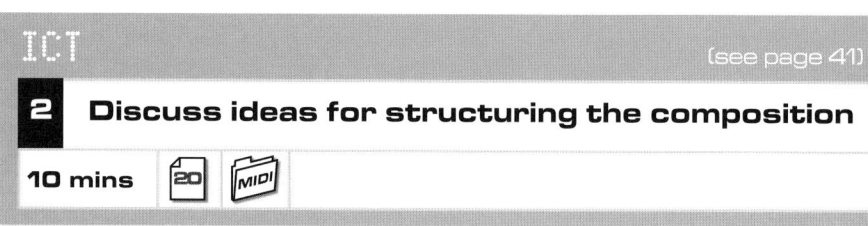

ICT (see page 41)

2 Discuss ideas for structuring the composition

10 mins

- Distribute copies of *Example composition plan* (printout 20), and explain the term **score**.

- Play *gladiator.mid* in the arrange window. Tell the class that this window is useful for viewing the structure, as you can see all the parts simultaneously.

- Play the file again and ask pupils to follow the song position line whilst listening, taking note of the different structural elements eg:
  - the piece starts with the bass ostinato alone;
  - the timpani and percussion enter with the drone;
  - the melody joins in after four repetitions of the bass ostinato;
  - hits appear later, increasing in frequency as the music builds to a climax;
  - all parts play together in unison at the climax.

- Discuss how viewing the score in this way could be useful to those working with ICT eg:
  - it is a useful record of ideas to remember for next lesson;
  - it shows time passing and scene changes in the trailer, which could help pupils make effective structural decisions;
  - it shows how the piece evolves and when each cliché begins and ends.

RETURN TO ACTIVITY 3 (page 41)

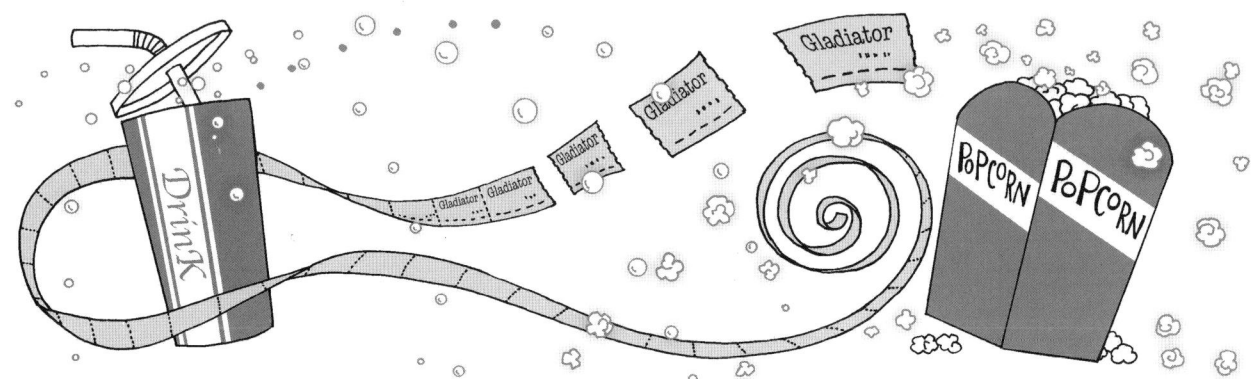

LESSON 5
COMPLETING THE STRUCTURE

ICT *(see page 41)*

3 Groups develop the structure of their composition

15 mins

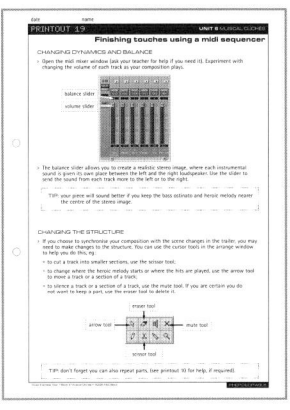

Printout 19: Finishing touches using a midi sequencer

- Pupils develop the structure of their composition using *Finishing touches using a midi sequencer* (printout 19).

- Demonstrate how to open the midi mixer window. (This is usually done from one of the menus at the top of the screen, eg the Panels or Windows menu.) You will see a volume slider for each track. If possible, label each slider as illustrated on printout 19.

- Encourage pupils to enhance the mood of their composition by:
  - using the volume sliders to change the volume level of each track whilst playing the composition, so that each instrument can be heard clearly;
  - changing the volume of a track during the course of the piece;
  - making adjustments to the left/right balance of each track to create an effective stereo image.

TEACHING TIPS

The time in the arrange window is shown in bars and beats, not seconds. Some sequencers allow the time to be displayed in either hours/minutes/seconds or bars/beats – consult your sequencer manual for more information. If your sequencer allows, you may wish to change the setting to make it easier for pupils to mark the scene changes.

Changes to the stereo image are only audible if the composition is played over a stereo sound system. Subtle changes to the left and right positioning of instruments are most effective.

◀◀ RETURN TO ACTIVITY 4   *(page 42)*

ICT *(see page 42)*

4 Pupils finalise their composition plan

5 mins

- Display *Assessment criteria* (printout 16). Revise the level descriptions and emphasise the importance of pupils' compositions having a clear structure.

- Pupils should finalise any structural decisions and then save their work.

EXTENSION ACTIVITY

If possible, allow groups to practise their composition in time with the trailer (video clip 5). A 5-4-3-2-1 countdown is provided at the start of the trailer so they know when to start.

TEACHING TIP

Synchronising the video and sequencer playback may need some rehearsal. The pupil starting the sequencer will need to identify the exact point near the beginning of the video at which to press PLAY on the sequencer.

◀◀ RETURN TO PLENARY   *(page 42)*

Lesson 6 — Performance

OBJECTIVES
By the end of the lesson pupils should:
- understand the clichés used in music for action film trailers;
- be able to perform their composition to the rest of the class.

OUTCOMES
Pupils:
- perform their composition in front of the class in time with the trailer;
- assess and evaluate their own and other pupils' compositions.

RESOURCES

CD-ROM
- Presentation
- Video clip 5
- Printouts 1–2, 16, 21–23
- Teacher information (optional)
- Midi files (optional)

INSTRUMENTS
- Untuned and tuned instruments (optional)
- Pupils bring in instruments from home (optional)
- Timpani tuned to D and A (optional)
- Electronic keyboards (optional)

ICT
- Whiteboard or computer and data projector
- Midi sequencer software (optional)
- Recording/filming equipment (optional)

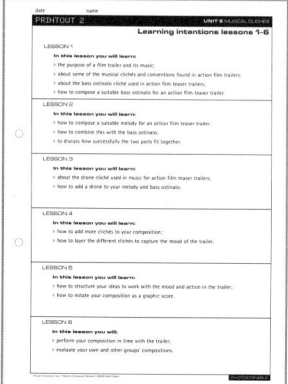

Printout 2: Learning intentions lessons 1–6

Focus
5 mins — Presentation

- Discuss the learning intentions for this lesson using the presentation on the CD-ROM or printout 2.

- Using *Programme notes* (printout 22), discuss the programme notes pupils wrote for homework, inviting groups to explain how they have made their composition fit the mood of the *Gladiator* trailer.

- Display *Assessment criteria* (printout 16) and revise the level descriptions.

1. Pupils rehearse their composition with the Gladiator trailer

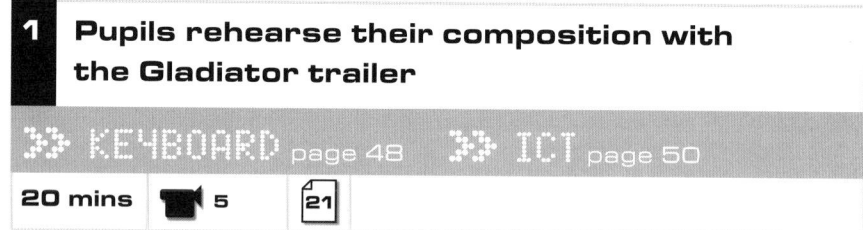

KEYBOARD page 48   **ICT** page 50
20 mins

- Pupils work in their groups to revise their composition. Ensure that they have copies of their *Composition plan* (printout 21) to refer to. They should also:
  - have all the instruments they require for their composition to hand;
  - know who is performing which part;
  - practise each part in turn with the bass ostinato making sure they are all confident about what they are performing and when;
  - practise performing all parts together, incorporating all the musical decisions they have made.

- Give each group the opportunity to practise their composition in time with the *Gladiator* trailer (video clip 5).

- As pupils work, remind them to think about performing their composition so that it really captures the mood of the trailer.

- Suggest pupils take it in turns to listen to their group while they are playing and feed back on balance, dynamics and mood.

TEACHING TIP
Circulate around the class as they work and help pupils to play their different parts in time with each other.

LESSON 6
PERFORMANCE

2 Groups perform their composition to the class

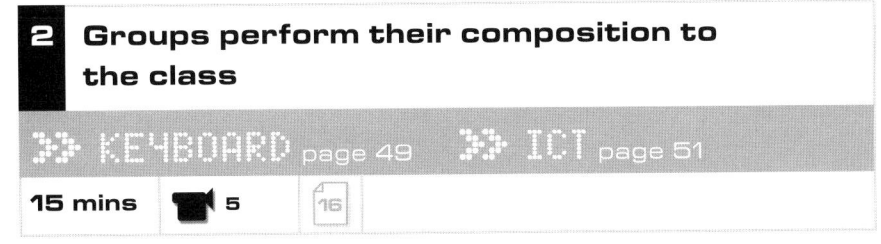

>> KEYBOARD page 49   **>> ICT** page 51

15 mins   🎥 5   📄 16

- Each group performs their composition to the class alongside the *Gladiator* trailer (video clip 5). After each performance, invite the class to provide constructive feedback for each composition. They might like to consider:
  - whether they think the composition captured the mood of the trailer;
  - whether there was a balanced sound;
  - whether there was clear evidence that the group had considered dynamics, structure, timbre and texture;
  - whether the different parts fitted together well.

EXTENSION ACTIVITY
Record or film each group, if possible, and then let them hear their composition whilst watching the trailer. Encourage each group to comment on which musical aspects of their work they are most pleased with.

TEACHING TIP
Pupils might find it useful to have copies of *Assessment criteria* (printout 16) to refer to.

ASSESSMENT FOR LEARNING

- Who is able to make a clear summary of evidence to match the assessment criteria?
- Who is using the correct terminology?
- Who can explain their ideas and contributes well to their group's work?

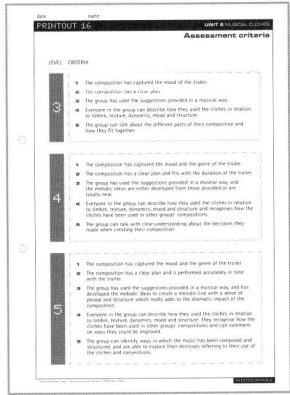

Printout 16: Assessment criteria

3 Groups assess their composition

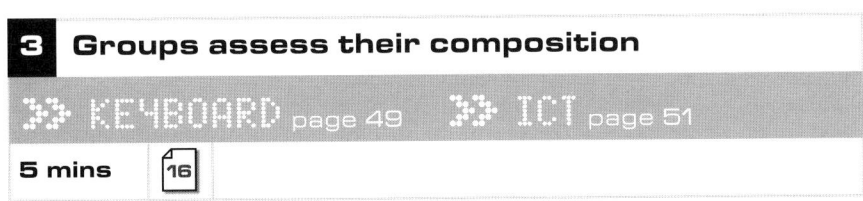

>> KEYBOARD page 49   **>> ICT** page 51

5 mins   📄 16

- Ask pupils to discuss which level they think their own composition reached, taking into account feedback from other groups and the level descriptions on *Assessment criteria* (printout 16).

- Each group then feeds back to the class on the level they have awarded their composition. Encourage them to support their assessment with evidence, and to discuss:
  - which musical ideas worked particularly well;
  - how their composition could have been improved;
  - the advantages and disadvantages of using acoustic instruments for their composition (*eg they may have had a limited range of instruments to choose from and it can be hard to coordinate all the layers. However, live acoustic instruments can be played with more expression, which can help increase the drama of the music*).

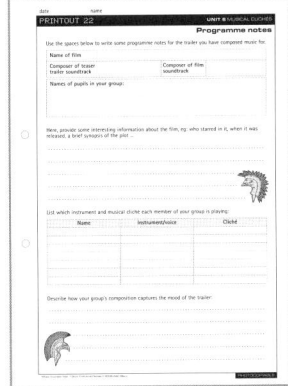

Printout 22: Programme notes

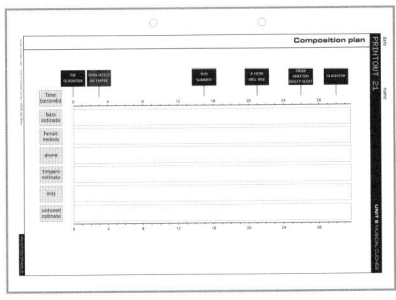

Printout 21: Composition plan

47

LESSON 6
PERFORMANCE

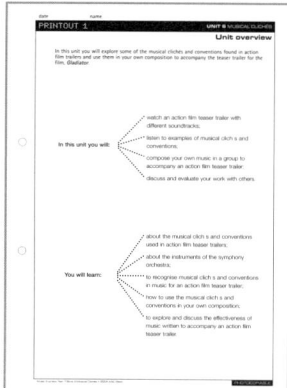

Printout 1: Unit overview

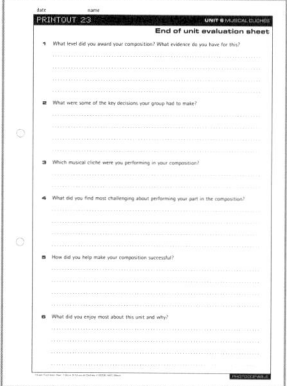

Printout 23: End of unit evaluation sheet

Plenary

5 mins | 1 | 23 | **Presentation**

- Remind pupils of the learning intentions for this unit using the presentation on the CD-ROM or printout 1.

- Discuss what pupils have enjoyed learning about most in this unit.

- Distribute copies of the *End of unit evaluation sheet* (printout 23) and explain how pupils should complete it for homework.

Homework 16 23

- Pupils complete the *End of unit evaluation sheet* (printout 23). They may also find it useful to have a copy of *Assessment criteria* (printout 16) to refer to.

KEYBOARD   (see page 46)

1 Pupils rehearse their composition with the Gladiator trailer

20 mins | 5 | 21

- Pupils work in their groups to revise their composition. Ensure that they have copies of their *Composition plan* (printout 21) to refer to. They should also:

  - have chosen their voices and have the relevant voice numbers to hand;
  - have decided which parts will be performed live and which recorded;
  - know who will operate the recorded tracks and volume control;
  - know in which registers the parts will be played;
  - ensure that each pupil can play their part correctly and knows when to enter;
  - be able to perform all parts together successfully, incorporating all the musical decisions they have made.

- Give each group the opportunity to practise their composition in time with the trailer (video clip 5).

- As the groups work, remind them to think about performing their composition so that it really captures the mood of the trailer.

- Suggest pupils take it in turns to listen to their group while they are playing and feed back on balance, dynamics and mood.

TEACHING TIP
Circulate round each group as they work and help pupils practise playing their different parts in time with each other.

« RETURN TO ACTIVITY 2   (page 47)

LESSON 6
PERFORMANCE

KEYBOARD (see page 47)

2 Groups perform their composition to the class

15 mins · 5 · 16

- Each group performs their composition to the class alongside the *Gladiator* trailer (video clip 5). After each performance, invite the class to provide constructive feedback for each composition. They might like to consider:
  - whether they think the composition enhanced the mood of the trailer;
  - how well the music flowed if there was a mixture of live and pre-recorded tracks;
  - whether there was a balanced sound;
  - whether there was clear evidence that the group had considered dynamics, structure, timbre and texture;
  - the advantages and disadvantages of using keyboards for this particular composition task *(eg on the one hand, keyboards have a large range of voices to choose from and it is easy to play in different registers; however it can be hard to coordinate all the layers, especially if some are recorded and some are played live. Also, not all keyboards can record which could limit the number of different parts that can be played)*.

EXTENSION ACTIVITY
Record or film each group if possible, and then let them hear their own composition whilst watching the trailer. Encourage each group to comment on which musical aspects they are most pleased with.

TEACHING TIP
Pupils might find it useful to have copies of **Assessment criteria** (printout 16) to refer to as they work.

RETURN TO ACTIVITY 3 (page 47)

KEYBOARD (see page 47)

3 Groups assess their composition

5 mins · 16

- Ask pupils to discuss which level they think their own composition reached, taking into account feedback from other groups and the level descriptions on *Assessment criteria* (printout 16).

- Each group then feeds back to the class on the level they would award their composition. Encourage them to support their assessment with evidence, and to discuss:
  - which musical ideas worked particularly well;
  - how their composition could have been improved;
  - whether the use of keyboards impacted on the success of their composition (see activity 2) and if so, how.

RETURN TO PLENARY (page 48)

LESSON 6
PERFORMANCE

ICT (see page 46)

1 Pupils rehearse their composition with the Gladiator trailer

20 mins • 5 • MIDI

- Pupils work in their groups to revise their composition. Ensure that they have:
  - made any final changes to the structure of their arrangement;
  - decided who is responsible for starting and stopping the sequencer and/or video clip;
  - rehearsed any changes to dynamics or balance which take place during the composition and know which member of the group will make these changes;
  - set the volume on the sound playback equipment to an appropriate level.

- Give pupils the opportunity to practise their composition in time with the *Gladiator* trailer (video clip 5).

- As the pupils work, remind them to think about performing their composition so that it really captures the mood of the trailer.

- Suggest pupils listen to their composition and discuss balance, dynamics and mood as they work.

TEACHING TIP
Synchronising the video and sequencer playback may need some rehearsal. The pupil starting the sequencer will need to identify the exact point near the beginning of the video at which to press PLAY on the sequencer.

« RETURN TO ACTIVITY 2 (page 47)

LESSON 6
PERFORMANCE

2 Groups perform their composition to the class

15 mins

- Each group performs their composition to the class alongside the *Gladiator* trailer (video clip 5).

- After each performance, invite the class to provide constructive feedback for each composition. They might like to consider:
  - whether they think the composition enhanced the mood of the trailer;
  - whether there was a balanced sound;
  - whether there was clear evidence that the group had considered dynamics, structure, timbre and texture;
  - whether the composition had a clear plan;
  - the advantages and disadvantages of using ICT for their composition *(eg a sequencer makes it easy to record, save and edit ideas; pupils can layer ideas to try out different textures and structures and can experiment with numerous different timbres. However, midi sounds cannot precisely replicate the sound of acoustic instruments; it is not possible to develop ideas through group improvisation and the spontaneity and energy of a live performance is lost).*

EXTENSION ACTIVITY
Record or film each group, and then let them hear their composition with the trailer. Encourage each group to comment on which musical aspects they are most pleased with.

TEACHING TIP
Pupils might find it useful to have copies of *Assessment criteria* (printout 16) to refer to.

 **RETURN** TO ACTIVITY 3 (page 47)

3 Groups assess their composition

5 mins

- Ask pupils to discuss which level they think their own composition reached, taking into account feedback from other groups and the level descriptions on *Assessment criteria* (printout 16).

- Each group feeds back to the class on the level they would award their composition. Encourage them to support their assessment with evidence, and to discuss:
  - which musical ideas worked particularly well;
  - how their composition could have been improved;
  - whether the use of ICT impacted on the success of their composition (see activity 2) and if so, how.

 **RETURN** TO PLENARY (page 48)

Gladiator demo

Will Taylor

GLOSSARY

arrange window — The main window on a sequencer that displays the whole song arrangement.

chord — Two or more notes played at the same time.

drone — A sustained tone, often in the bass, played throughout much or all of a piece of music. Drones are used in music all over the world, including Indian raga and British folk music.

dynamics — The volume at which music is played. Volume is often described using Italian words, eg *forte, piano, mezzo forte, mezzo piano, crescendo, diminuendo* etc.

freeware — Software freely available without charge.

genre — A type or category. Pop, folk, classical and jazz are all musical genres.

hit — Hits are used to provide emphasis points in a piece of music and can be played by orchestras, untuned percussion or special FX.

left/right marker — A marked point in the sequencer arrange window. This is sometimes called a left/right locator.

midi — Musical Instrument Digital Interface – a language that allows compatible software and hardware to communicate.

midi mixer — A window that allows mute, solo and volume changes for each sequencer track.

musical cliché — A phrase or convention which is overused in a particular genre of music and is therefore predictable. From the French 'clicher', meaning 'to stereotype'.

mute — To silence a sequencer track.

note — A symbol used in staff notation to indicate the pitch and duration of a sound.

ostinato — A short repeated rhythmic or melodic pattern.

pitch — The complete range of sounds in music from the highest to the lowest. A general rule of thumb in music is the larger the instrument, the lower its pitch.

phrase — A section of a larger melody.

pulse — A steady beat.

real time input — Recording music into a sequencer by playing notes on a midi keyboard.

register — A specific range of a voice or instrument.

rhythm patterns — Combinations of different note lengths organised into patterns.

scale	An arrangement of specific notes played in order of pitch from the lowest to the highest (or vice versa). We choose notes for compositions from scales; scales therefore give character to music.
score	A printed or sometimes handwritten depiction of a musical work.
sequencer	Software for recording, composing and arranging music, which can have midi or audio tracks.
shareware	Software subject to a registration fee.
SMF	Standard Midi File – a basic midi file format that can be recognised by different software packages.
soundcard	A hardware device installed in a computer which creates the sound output. It often includes a midi interface.
staccato	Notes which are played short and detached.
step time input	Recording music into a sequencer one note at a time, for example, by using the pen tool.
stereo image	The position of sounds between left and right loudspeakers.
structure	How music is put together. This may refer to how a piece of music divides into sections, eg beginning, middle and end.
syncopation	Instead of accenting the strong beat (eg: <u>1</u> 2 <u>3</u> 4), syncopated music accents the weak beats – the off-beats (eg: 1 <u>2</u> 3 <u>4</u> or 1 <u>+</u> 2 <u>+</u> 3 <u>+</u> 4 <u>+</u>).
tempo	The speed of the steady beat. Tempo is often described using Italian words, eg *allegro, andante, moderato, presto, vivace* etc.
texture	The number of performers in a piece. Some pieces are written for a set number of performers and these create particular textures, eg soloist, duet, trio, quartet and quintet.
timbre	The unique characteristic sound of each instrument. Every instrument, including the human voice, has its own particular sound.
tremolo	The fast repetition of a note, often by strings or percussion instruments.
triplet	A group of three notes of equal length performed in the time of two.
voice	An individual instrument sound or special effect on a keyboard. Most voices are grouped into categories or families and printed on the keyboard panel.

ACKNOWLEDGEMENTS

The authors and publishers would like to thank the following teachers, consultants and colleagues who assisted in the preparation of this book:

Jamie Acton-Bond, Stephen Chadwick, Anne Cooper, Tatiana Demidova, Claire Hall, Maureen Hanke, Erika Jenkins, Matthew Jones, Harriet Lowe, Jocelyn Lucas, Susan McIntyre, Carla Moss, Neil Pardoe, Cath Rasbash, Jeanne Roberts, Sheena Roberts, Jane Sebba, Ian Shepherd, Sarah Smith, Philomena Taylor, Rebecca Taylor, Abigail Walmsley and Emily Wilson.

The following have kindly granted permission for the inclusion of their copyright materials in *Music Express Year 7 Book 6: Musical clichés***:**

Anvil of Crom by Basil Poledouris © 1982 Universal City Studios Inc.

Gladiator © 2000 Dreamworks LLC and Universal Studios. Courtesy of Universal Studios Licensing LLLP

Gladiator demo by Will Taylor © 2006 Will Taylor. Worldwide rights administered by A&C Black Publishers Ltd.

Movement 1 from *Mythodea*. Performed by Vangelis. Courtesy of Sony BMG Music Entertainment (UK) Ltd. Licensed by Sony BMG Commercial Markets UK.

On earth as it is in heaven from *The Mission* by Ennio Morricone. Licensed courtesy of Virgin Records Ltd.

The Society Raffles by Stephen Chadwick © 2003 Stephen Chadwick. Worldwide rights administered by A&C Black Publishers Ltd.

Every effort has been made to trace and acknowledge copyright owners. If any right has been omitted, the publishers offer their apologies and will rectify this in subsequent editions following notification.

Photocopying – only the pages marked photocopiable may be freely photocopied and only for educational purposes for use in the school or educational establishment for which this resource was purchased. Within these terms in this resource you are permitted to photocopy the printouts on the CD-ROM.

Single Use licence – please note that the copyright holders have licensed the material in this publication for single use only. In the case of the midi files, permission is granted to download the files onto more than one computer or a network server for classroom use only, provided that after the unit has been taught the files are deleted. If you have any queries about the manner in which you may use the material, please contact music@acblack.com.